To my friend,
Dot.

Blessings

D0106022

# IMAGINING
## THE SMALL CHURCH

# IMAGINING
## THE SMALL CHURCH

*Celebrating a Simpler Path*

Steve Willis

The Alban Institute
www.alban.org

Copyright © 2012 by The Alban Institute. All rights reserved. This material may not be photocopied or reproduced in any way without written permission. Go to www.alban.org/permissions.asp or write to the address below.

The Alban Institute
2121 Cooperative Way, Suite 100
Herndon, VA 20171

Unless otherwise noted, all Scripture quotations are from the New Revised Standard Version of the Bible, copyright © 1989, Division of Christian Education of the National Council of the Churches of Christ in the United States of America, and are used by permission.

Library of Congress Cataloging-in-Publication Data

Willis, Steve.
  Imagining the small church : celebrating a simpler path / Steve Willis.
    p. cm.
  Includes bibliographical references.
  ISBN 978-1-56699-433-0
  1. Small churches.  I. Title.
  BV637.8.W55 2012
  253--dc23
                                    2012029467


12    13    14    15    16        VG        5    4    3    2    1

# Contents

# Foreword

In *Imagining the Small Church*, pastor, writer, and lover of small things Steve Willis takes us on a narrative and imaginative journey. Some readers will have a sense that what Willis is describing simply names what they have already known in their hearts about their small churches. For them the journey will cover some familiar ground, explore some territory from a fresh angle, but deposit them nearly home again, hopefully with just a bit more awareness and appreciation. For others, though, Willis will take them on a long journey to a far and foreign place. They probably won't bother to finish reading it, and they will miss his invitation to find pastoring a small church "extremely rewarding and meaningful." They will find this a strange book—weird, off-center, and impractical; unlivable in the twenty-first century and undesirable in any event. This is because Willis is taking on the ethos, the values of our age, and claiming that it needn't be so. We can live on a different basis. We can live on the basis of gospel values. The table of contents sets out his agenda in bullet form: periphery, simplicity, limits, creation, belonging, bills, and imagination. The values of our dominant culture can very nearly be summed up in these oppositional qualities: centrality, complexity, unrestraint, consumption, freedom from commitment, wealth, and drudgery.

Let us posit Willis's premise that small churches and small places more nearly incarnate gospel values, and then consider what dominoes fall from that posture. First, that puts spiritually healthy small churches and people in at least a countercultural, if not an anticultural, position. Somebody important once said, "You cannot serve both God and mammon." This is reality. And it is a good thing. So let us stop with the grief and the regret. Let us see through the illusion of American culture as godly. Let us proclaim, "The Emperor is naked," and offer some clothing. Let us stop whining about cultural shifts and start witnessing to the transforming power of God (maybe by experiencing it first!). I pastored a small church for twenty years. For the past seventeen years as a denominational official, I have visited hundreds of small churches. I wish I had a nickel for every Christian who lamented the current state of their smaller and smaller church, saying that they are unable to compete with the town sports league on Sunday mornings. What? Society owes us support? Society owes us young people? Society owes us new members? Society owes us an unencumbered time slot? Get over it. Society has already co-opted us by not taxing our real estate. In that sense, society has already done too much for us. Society is not our ally in the maintenance of our religious preferences. Society is our opposition. We are to *counter* the culture, not by mandating our will but by infiltration: yeasting.

If we are countercultural, then two things follow. We must have integrity. Our members must be maturing. Our congregations must be places of love, affirmation, correction, and righteousness. Our congregations must be places where people learn how to deal with interpersonal conflict, overcome racism, break free of addictions, steward creation, and grow their souls. Our congregations must be places where these values are practiced: periphery, simplicity, limits,

creation, belonging, bills, and imagination. Our congregations must be places where these things are opposed: centrality, complexity, unrestraint, consumption, freedom from
commitment, wealth, and drudgery. Our congregations must
be places where pain, loss, sacrifice, and grief are borne con-
structively and transformed into progress toward God's purpose. Don't we worship one who did not avoid the cross but
bore its pain on our behalf? Or do we actually worship Uncle
Sam or Adam Smith or Horatio Alger or Dionysus? To be
countercultural, we must stand clearly and fully in our alternative values, embodying them at a high level.

And to complement integrity we must also have compassion in action. Today we are calling it being *missional.*
Outreach, caring, serving, ministry; do we have as many acts
of kindness as names for it? Well, whatever we call it, let us
be about it. Remember those lamenting churches? Well . . .
one church was different; it didn't complain about Sunday
morning sports leagues. It prayed for them! The pastor asked
for prayers for Deacon "Jones," since he was at the soccer
league. Were we praying for him to repent, I wondered? Later
the pastor told me the story. The deacon went with his son
to the season's first game and, just before the start, pulled
him aside. They prayed for safe play and sportsmanship. The
next week the same, except that two friends asked what was
happening, and upon being told, asked if "your father could
pray for us, too." The third week, most of the team came
to the sideline for prayer. The fourth week, the coach asked
the deacon if he would be the team chaplain. So now every
week during the season, the deacon has a ministry—and the
church, far from lamenting, is praying him on!

Because our values differ from society's and because society is a lot bigger, more powerful, and unforgiving of opposition, it may behoove us to construct our own vision,

developmental paths, and reinforcements, God being our helper. As people convinced that the healthy small church is God's yeast, how do we go about getting and keeping our ferment? I don't presume to have many answers, but I am pretty sure that these are some of the key questions we must address if the small church is to play the crucial role God has in mind for us to counter culture:

+ How can small-church folk add depth to their spiritual structures?
+ How can a local church's traditions be both affirmed and transcended?
+ How can small churches allow more people to enter their *koinonia*?
+ How can small-church people feel as energized—or at least as comfortable—doing things outside the church's walls as they are inside?
+ How can personal, spiritual maturity become our watchword?
+ How can we get out from under the costs of full-time, paid clergy and building ownership?
+ How can small-church people learn again to delight in the cries and even the dirty diapers of spiritual babies?

The small church has been made by God to be exactly the right scale and form to incarnate alternative values that can bring life to people and justice to communities. Somebody who was pretty important said, "Choose this day whom you will serve."

Tony G. Pappas
Executive Minister
American Baptist Churches of Massachusetts

# *Preface*

Small church is a wonderful and beautiful way of doing church. It must be because the vast majority of Christian churches are small and always have been. In my own denomination we have approximately 10,500 churches and somewhere around 7,000 of these are small churches. Yet most of what we hear and read about church comes from voices amplified to large audiences. Published sermons come from tall-steeple preachers. Denominational church-planning strategies and curricula come from large, programmatic church environments. In the media, news stories about the church come from megachurches. Yet every twenty or thirty years the small church is rediscovered. Of course, it never went away. The small church simply continues to love the people and places where it resides, telling the good news story of Jesus Christ to generation after generation.

I should say a few things about what I mean by *small church*. Usually a small church is defined as a congregation with one hundred or fewer average participants in worship. This definition is helpful because very significant differences begin to appear when a church surpasses the one-hundred-person threshold. Yet this definition still leaves a great diversity of many different churches in many different contexts. Variety is the norm among these churches, and the uniqueness of each congregation reflects its distinct place in

the world. Yet whether the small church is in an older urban neighborhood, a newer suburb, or a mountain hollow, it
finds its unique resiliency in the loving depth of its people's
relationships and its commitment to the special place where
it resides.

When I began inquiring about ordained ministry as a pastor in the Presbyterian Church (USA) in 1990, I did not know
that my life's vocation would be as a pastor of a small church.
Now in my eighteenth year as a small-church solo pastor, I
do know how the small church can capture one's love and
affection. The caring, faithfulness, and tenacity of this particular way of being and doing church has changed how I see
God at work in the world and what I think is important for
myself and my family.

This book is a way of bearing witness to what I have seen
God doing in small churches. It is a way of lifting up the
stories of people in these churches who give so much of themselves in loving people and places. Even more so, I hope to
argue that the present state of mainline Protestantism on the
sidelines of culture means that the small church has much
to teach us right now. We in denominational Protestantism
are getting smaller every day. What does this mean? What
does the future hold for us? One way to imagine our changing situation is by listening to the stories of churches that are
used to being small and accustomed to living at the margins.

This book boasts no ten or fifteen steps to a successful
small church. Instead, I hope to encourage you to give up on
steps altogether and even to give up on success, at least how
success is usually measured. I also hope to help the reader
imagine the small church differently; to see with new eyes the
joys and pleasures of living small and sustainably. For many
years I have strained to see the small church through the eyes

of the people who love her so deeply, because I think they see the small church more similarly to the way God does. What they see are the faces of people and the specifics of place. The words they use to describe what they see include *love, belonging,* and *faithfulness.* Why in the world would we prefer steps and success over these?

I have pastored small churches in rural, town, and urban settings. The stories of the people you will meet in this book come from the rural environments of southern Appalachia and eastern Washington State. These stories and insights are drawn from healthy and vital small churches that have been small through the entirety of their congregational history. These are the folks I have known best and the places with which I have fallen in love. Their stories are meant to inspire the reader to attend closely to the wonder of God's grace alive in the people and places of small-church life, wherever they may be—city, town, or country. I also hope this book is helpful for people who come from large, programmatic churches yet work with small churches in denominational or ecumenical settings.

I am a Presbyterian pastor; therefore much of my language and church jargon come from my own denominational church family. Please feel free to substitute your own church family language when you hear me use words like *elder* (church officer), *session* (church board), or *presbytery* (denominational judicatory). People always experience church in all its minute particularities. A whole bunch of wonderful flavors of church are out there. Whether you are chocolate chip cookie dough, raspberry sorbet, or banana nut, I hope that you will find this book tasty.

Finally, a few words of thanks. Thank you to the small churches that I have been privileged to serve for showing me that we never outgrow the most basic Christian priority, which is love. Especially thank you to the joyful, loving, faithful people of Virginia Presbyterian Church in Buchanan where I serve now. Thank you to the friends and colleagues from whom I have learned this love for people in small churches and small places. Especially thank you to Larry and Margaret Menz, Charles Stewart, Dave Helmbock, Bill Reynolds, John Michaelson, George and Micki Weisbarth, Jerry and Dee Hargitt, Mike and Sandee Meade, Matt and Janine Goodrich, Bonnie Evans, Michelle Bartel, Tony Pappas, Kim Steinhorst, and Mary Harris Todd. Thanks to Tony and Michelle for reading and giving input on chapters of this book. Thanks to my editor, Fritz Gutwein, who has been such a great help. Thanks to all the past and present friends of Lectio Jubilate. Thanks to my mom, Betty, an officer in her small, Presbyterian, North Carolina mountain church and an unfailing advocate for her children. For her constant support and understanding, all my thanks and love go to my wife, Amy, my true companion. This book is dedicated to my wonderful children, Nate and Cate, who have been loved and nurtured in the small church. Nate and Cate, I hope that as you grow up you will remember that small is beautiful.

# CHAPTER I

# *Periphery*

Moses was keeping the flock of his father-in-law Jethro, the priest of Midian; he led his flock *beyond the wilderness*, and came to Horeb, the *mountain* of God.

Exodus 3:1 (italics mine)

*My grandmother, Mae Huskins, always seemed to me a rather stern woman, even with her fiery red hair and piercing blue eyes. We called her Mama, and her heavy, black King James Bible rested on the coffee table in the family room and not on her bedside table like my Mema Willis. I always thought her quiet severity was related to her religion, which was passed down from her father, the stoic Baptist preacher John Googe. But it makes more sense, looking back, that living much of one's life without running water or electricity can make a tough nut out of anyone.*

*"Your mama sure knew how to run a restaurant" was the word that I heard over and over again from her neighbors and friends. She was a remarkable Southern cook, but I had a sense that these remarks meant more than praise for her fried rainbow trout, creamed corn, and coleslaw.*

*In the bedroom hallway hung a picture of her as a striking, lithe, beautiful, young woman as she sat weaving on a tall, wooden, foot-pedaled loom. Later I discovered that picture came from a 1935 book written about rural, western*

North Carolina folk entitled *Cabins in the Laurel*. The caption in the book underneath her picture simply reads, "The mountain girl is skillful and can turn her hand to anything."[1] The picture was taken where Mama had learned to weave, at the Penland School of Crafts.

In 1913 the Reverend Rufus Morgan, an Episcopalian priest just graduated from General Theological Seminary in New York, came to this most isolated county in North Carolina and started the Appalachian School. His sister Lucy Morgan graduated from a teachers' college in central Michigan. She helped start the Penland School of Crafts. Lucy's weaving skills were the beginning of the Penland School. Even before the school had a building, the first loom was hauled up the mountain and assembled on the front porch of Henry and Martha Willis's cabin. Rufus and Lucy had grown up in rural Murphy, North Carolina, and they left it for urban centers in the Northeast and Midwest for their formal educations. They returned to western North Carolina with new skills and learning to add to their love and appreciation for their own mountain culture.

Penland School taught weaving skills to young Appalachian women. These women learned together how to make and market their goods as far away as Chicago. Most importantly, the school gathered a variety of people from different backgrounds and experiences who worked together toward a common goal. Skills and learning from the wealthy, educated cities of New England and the Midwest were mixed with the local wisdom of folks from the Appalachian hollows and branches of western North Carolina. This creative mixture brought into being a remarkable community that has endured and still thrives as a place where people go to buy wonderful pottery and reflect on the nature of good work. Even today the license plates in the parking lot at the Penland School reveal people coming from all over the country.

Here is where Mama first began gathering the skills for running her restaurant, for running her business—mountain style.

Not long ago I was back in Mitchell County and sitting with my mother in the hospital as my stepfather was battling the effects of lung disease. One night a nurse came into the room and introduced herself. She and my mother went through the usual routine of chatting about names of family and people they knew. When the nurse found out my mother's maiden name was Huskins, she became quite excited to discover that Mom was Ed and Mae's daughter. She blurted out, "Well, I've heard lots of stories about them, from my daddy. He's Danny Young." After which there were hugs and holding hands and a phone call to Danny. In thirty minutes Dan, now sixty-plus years old, was in the hospital room talking about his teenage years working at Ed and Mae's restaurant.

Later that night Dan said to me, "Your mama sure knew how to run a restaurant. I remember so well working at the Circle." He spoke about what a character my papa was and how Ed welcomed customers and told stories and kept people coming back. But for years quietly and behind the scenes, Mae ran the business and hired more people than they needed. Some folks who couldn't get a job somewhere else found a home there. Everyone was important in this community and paid fairly and found a place to belong. Dan concluded, "I don't think they ever made much money, but the Circle Restaurant was kind of an institution that people here cared about for a long time."

> *Although I don't recall Mama and Papa ever talking about why they named the family restaurant the Circle, I suspect it had some meaning to them. Any Baptist preacher's daughter knew the words to the 1907 gospel hymn "Will the Circle Be Unbroken."*

In this story about my mama, the mountain folk are representatives of what farmer, poet, and agrarian writer Wendell Berry calls a *peripheral culture*; Rufus and Lucy Morgan's educational experiences in the urban Northeast and Midwest represent the influences of what he calls a *central culture*.[2] To quote Berry,

> These terms [center and periphery] appear to be plain enough, but as I am going to use them here they may need a little clarification. We can say, for example, that a land grant university is a center with a designated periphery which it is supposed to maintain and improve. Or an industrial city is a center with a periphery which it is bound to influence and which, according to its politics and power, it may either conserve or damage. Or a national or a state government is a center solemnly entrusted with a responsibility for peripheral places, but in general it extends its protections and favors to the commercial centers, which outvote or out-"contribute" the periphery. . . . It is useful because the dichotomy between center and periphery does in fact exist, as does the tendency of the center to be ignorant of the periphery.[3]

Many small churches live in a peripheral culture. These churches are very aware of the cultural differences between the center and the periphery. They have experienced the times that the central culture has negatively used its power and influence on them, trying to make these peripheral places look and act more like central-culture places. When central-culture institutions damage peripheral-culture institutions through abuse of power, the central culture becomes a dominant culture and peripheral culture becomes marginalized. Dominant culture demands uniformity and therefore does not understand the importance of peripheral culture. Both centers and peripheries are necessary and important for human civilization. As long as human beings need to govern themselves and create institutions and communicate, then there will be a need for central culture. And as long as human beings need to eat and clothe themselves and heat their homes, then there will be a need for peripheral culture. These two cultures are inherently interrelated. They depend on each other for their health and well-being. Yet as Berry writes, "the tendency of the center is to be ignorant of the periphery."

The dichotomy between center and periphery is not simply a division between urban and rural. Large populations of marginalized communities also reside in urban centers. With the massive shift away from an industrial economy in the United States, entire Midwestern cities have found themselves at a new periphery. And in rural communities, government policies since the end of World War II have forced small farms out of existence. In the wake of that damage, new agribusiness centers have appeared, dominating large areas of the rural landscape. All this is to say that the lines between center and periphery are not always clear. Much rural and small-town culture is peripheral culture, but not always. Some urban and suburban culture is central culture, but much of it is not. And both cultures are always changing, sometimes gaining power and influence and sometimes losing them.

Churches live and minister in these different cultures. Sometimes the churches have significant influence on the cultures in which they live. But the culture always has a powerful influence on how the people of these churches understand and perceive their world. Small churches are quite aware of the differences between central-culture congregations and peripheral-culture congregations. But often churches located in central cultures are not well aware of the differences. The central culture is simply assumed to be the way that things work. So voices in the center often assume that the voices at the periphery are simply not measuring up. From this dominant perspective, the differences are not viewed as differences in culture but as a failure of effort or education. When central-culture church power and influence fails to respect the differences and imposes itself on small peripheral churches, it causes damage to these congregations.

The dichotomy between central churches and peripheral churches, however, is not simply a division between large and small. Many large, programmatic churches are finding themselves on a new periphery. And a few small churches have power, resources, and influence well beyond their numbers. As mainline Protestantism has lost power and influence in the center of American culture, many churches are struggling to adapt to the change from being at the center to being at the periphery or even at the margin. Many denominational churches are confused because they are not sure where they are in the new cultural landscape. And their vivid memories of the past, when they sat squarely in the center, make it all the more difficult for them to see what is going on today. The advantage that many small churches have in this situation is a clear understanding of where they are—on the periphery.

Most clergy I know who pastor small churches are quite aware of their social location and of the differences between central- and peripheral-church cultures. We often move between the two worlds of our local church community and our denominational structures. Many of us have spent much time studying the languages and becoming bilingual in the tongues of these different worlds. It is necessary to speak in both the theological language of the denominational church culture and the practical, feeling faith-language of the small church. Knowing both of these languages yields fruit not unlike studying Greek and Hebrew to better understand the Scriptures. Small-church pastors also work hard to explain and assure the local church that the larger denominational structures are important for their long-term health. Then we pray that the "powers that be" do not attempt another strategy to "fix" the small, local congregation.

Many small-church clergy friends find it amusing, when it's not maddening, how our denominational cultures create new centers and peripheries within the larger church cultures themselves. We listen to some dominant church leaders complain about the way their churches are being mistreated by the changing American culture, and then they turn around and misuse their power and influence within the church family.

Fortunately, however, awareness about the differences between small and large churches is growing. Fewer mistaken assumptions are made that small churches are just less successful approximations of large churches. A growing literature about small-church life has helped the church center's awareness of the periphery. Now in most seminary bookstores one can find the little section in the corner labeled "Small-Church Ministry" that describes the experience of the majority of our churches. I have noticed a larger appreciation in denominational structures for those "willing" to serve small rural and urban congregations. Programs are now in place to help small-church pastors relieve their seminary debt and to provide financial assistance for pursuing further degrees and taking sabbaticals. These changes all reflect a welcome appreciation for the work of small churches.

So my purpose for adding my voice to all that has been written about the small church is not to complain about the way that central voices crowd out peripheral voices. Rather, I would like to point to the valuable resources of the small-church experience for those who lead in these settings and encourage other leaders who are considering doing ministry in small congregations. The following chapters are an attempt to describe the strengths and skills I have witnessed in small, peripheral churches and especially, and ironically, to argue for their importance in thinking about the future of mainline Protestantism.

An incredible amount of thinking and dreaming about the future of mainline Protestantism is going on. But most of this conversation about where the church is going does not concern itself with small-church life in small town or rural settings. This is true in part because future-oriented, reflective work is not a natural part of most small-church life. But it is also true because central church structures, wondering aloud about the future, most often hear only the voices that speak center-culture language. Books, conferences, webinars, and many resources well beyond my knowing are imagining the new day and planning for what may be emerging in the future. Quite honestly, I think that much of this is outstanding. I have a few clergy friends on the church's cutting edges, and I always find it educational and exciting to hear what dreams are being dreamt. I feel a deep gratitude for the gifts and intuition of these pioneers and pray for fruit to come from their extensive labors.

Yet if the church's past has anything to say about its future, then there is not just one future out there. Rather, the church will experience a great variety of futures. Our past teaches us that when the church has been in a peripheral culture position, variety has been the norm. The early church, before the rise of Emperor Constantine the Great, who adopted Christianity as the religion of the realm, exhibited great diversity of Christian practice. In our changing situation it is unwise to hope for one magical solution that will help us find our footing when the ground feels so unsure. Real, significant, and deep change is surely here, but it will still take time, patience, and love to guide communities of faith into the future, just as it always has.

After the printing press and the Gutenberg Bible radically changed the nature of Christianity, centuries passed before most churches had a mimeograph machine in the office. With the vast diversity of contexts in which churches carry out their mission, it would be difficult to believe that a large percentage are in a situation that could be described as cutting edge. While it is right and good that dreamers and pioneers should follow their calling, and all of us should listen to their voices, there is also the possibility that our anxiety about the future has led quite a few leaders into a frantic dabbling in new, untested techniques that do not serve all churches well.

Quite often I drive by the Peaks Presbyterian Church on my way to hike through the Blue Ridge Mountains. The little, white clapboard church sits in a beautiful setting, looking up to Sharp Top and Flat Top Mountains of the Peaks of Otter, among the highest elevations in Virginia. This congregation has always been a small country church since it was founded in 1761. It has survived the Revolutionary War, the trauma of our nation's Civil War, the Great War to end all wars, the Second World War, Vietnam, the culture wars of the sixties, and now continues its ministry today. The Peaks Church's beginnings hearken back to a time that had a quite different understanding of church and pastoral leadership.

During the period when the Peaks Church came into existence, stability was the norm for ministers, who most often pastored the same church their entire ministerial life. A study of Congregationalist ministers who graduated from Yale College during this era shows the difference between then and now. Robert W. Lynn and James W. Fraser, church analysts who in 1977 contributed to one of the first books written specifically about the small church, summarize the differences.

> The eighteenth-century New England Congregationalists did not view the successful pastor as one who changed churches. That 7 percent with more than two pastorates consisted of the "ne'er to do wells." The situation was precisely the reverse of today, that is, Congregational pastors of that time looked upon themselves as holding identical offices with identical problems. There were no essential spiritual distinctions between the minister who labored in a small Connecticut hamlet and the pastor of the prominent church in New Haven or Boston.[4]

Until the late nineteenth-century, the small church had been the normative model for congregations in any context: city, town, or country. Not until the construction of public mass-transit systems in major urban areas had the large church, as we now know it, been a possibility. Tony Pappas, American

Baptist Area Minister in Massachusetts and small-church advocate, describes it this way.

> So for the first time in human history, thousands of people could get to a one- or two-hour event and get home for lunch! So large churches, big steeples, big pulpits, Old Firsts came into being. As we think of them today, large churches have only been around for a little over a century—only 5% of the history of our faith.[5]

The large church's development in major urban centers also coincided with the growing American industrial economy. The prototype for the megachurch was the famous Plymouth Church of the Pilgrims in Brooklyn, New York, which built an unmatched membership of two thousand people. The business entrepreneurs John Tasker Howard and Henry Chandler Bowen were the businessmen behind the congregation's formation. Spiritual as well as financial incentives provided the impetus for building supersized churches. Debby Applegate describes this dynamic in her biography of Plymouth Church's first pastor, Henry Ward Beecher, who came to New York in 1847.

> On a practical level, a popular church was an excellent investment. It was exempt from taxes, its revenues were regular, it was unlikely to chisel or default, and it brought up the real estate values of the neighborhood, creating more opportunities for wise investors to make money. The church paid the owners rent or a mortgage with a profitable interest rate, and they could make extra money by hiring out the building for speeches, concerts, meetings, and other entertainments during the week.[6]

But before parishioners could travel by car, train, or Beecher boats to church on Sunday, churches had been small. The normative model for the vast majority of church history has been the small church, and the percentages show that this is still true today.

Of course, today is not the eighteenth or nineteenth centuries, and much has changed, including changes both welcome and lamentable. If we consider the church's position in the larger culture and the influence and power of the mainline Protestant church on society, things today more closely resemble 1761 than 1950. By this I mean that denominational Christianity has found itself in the periphery of the dominant American culture. Even our central-culture churches have found themselves at a new periphery. We have experienced a loss of social influence and status in the culture and a loss of resources. As much of a shock as it is to our system, we know that the church's position in any culture ebbs and flows. We have little control over whether we are flowing or whether we are ebbing.

So I want to tell the stories of peripheral rural churches I have known well. These churches are familiar with living in the ebbing times and amid peripheral settings, and yet they embody an abundance of life and love. Almost a decade ago my family made the decision to return to small, peripheral church life. We left a large urban center for the rural countryside. And we left a wealthy, professional church culture for a scrappy working-class congregation. My return journey was an experience of recovering love and passion for day-to-day ministry. I went home, but now with new eyes that could see more clearly the tenacious sustainability of these small, peripheral congregations that persevere through love of people and places. These churches have had experience and have developed skills at continuing a ministry without a section of cheerleaders shouting them on. These surprising communities of faith have not only survived but also continue to be vital communities, even amid marginalization, lack of resources, and sometimes the absence of pastoral leadership. During a time when the dominant culture demands that the overbearing solution to every problem is the market, these peripheral churches have rejected marketing and business strategies as incongruent with their mission. And yet they continue to faithfully persevere as they love people and places, making their witness to the living God of Jesus Christ.

When I think back to my grandmother's restaurant and learning at the Penland School of Crafts, I am amazed at how many different people came together to shape her experience. The Penland community exhibited a unique mix of central and peripheral cultural perspectives with values and learning from each culture. Rufus and Lucy Morgan left the comforts of home to travel and learn from central-culture educational institutions. When this learning was mixed with the skills and perspectives of rural, western North Carolina mountain people, a rich, tenacious, lovely community came to be.

Today there is knowledge to explore that comes from healthy, sustainable, rural churches. We need to start thinking the other way around about where we are in the culture and what place we inhabit. Mainline Protestantism has grown comfortable and accustomed to the center, but we need to relearn gifts and skills from the periphery. Our social location is changing—really, it has already dramatically changed. So our learning needs to change as well.

I wish and pray for a time in the church that values and grows from the insight, experience, resources, and stories of all our diverse and varied ministries. A more in-depth collaboration among and learning from both central- and peripheral-church ways of being will provide needed perspectives and skills for living into an ever-changing future. Sharing our diverse voices and gifts can help us all remember that it is the sovereign, gracious God of Jesus Christ who is the center of our life together.

# CHAPTER 2

# *Simplicity*

*A faithful stewardship that shuns ostentation and seeks proper use of the gifts of God's creation.*
Book of Order, Presbyterian Church (USA)[1]

*If there is a pertinent modern question, it is "How much is enough?"*
Bill McKibben, *The Bill McKibben Reader*[2]

Any advocate for the small church is an advocate for simplicity. The Christian attribute and discipline of simplicity may be one of the most needful ideas for the American mainline church to reclaim as it faces the future. Because what I have seen described as simplicity in the dominant culture sometimes makes my head spin, I will illustrate simplicity by drawing a contrast.

Almost two decades ago now, I went on a two-week tour of different churches of varying denominations in very different parts of the Southeast. We were a group of seminarians studying small, medium, and large churches that were situated in rural, suburban, and urban contexts. The size and setting of each church was viewed with appreciation and sympathy. The professor's goal was to produce ministers who grew the membership of their churches, regardless of the congregation's size or context. The two-week traveling course through the Southeast was a course on evangelism for mainline Protestants.

The course reached its climax when we arrived at our final visit, a megachurch that boasted more than ten thousand members on the rolls. We were also in one of the most prosperous and influential neighborhoods in the entire Southeast. Even for those not planning to minister in large-church settings, the experience made a lasting impression.

I was assigned on Sunday morning to attend a class specifically designed for young, single people in their twenties. "Now this will be interesting," I thought, because twenty-somethings are the seemingly impossible age for the church to reach. When I walked into the meeting room, I was surprised to find twenty people already gathering and talking about their week. In the next five minutes, another fifteen arrived to make a group of thirty-five young people who gathered to study the Scriptures and talk about their faith. I was pleasantly stunned.

After everyone had poured a nice cup of coffee and taken their seats, we started around the large circle introducing ourselves. One person after another had a similar introduction.

"Hi, I'm Jill Johnson. I graduated from Emory University and I work at Arthur Andersen."

"Hello, I'm Scott McDonald. I graduated from Duke University and Duke Law School. I'm a lawyer at a firm downtown."

"Good morning, I'm David Graham. I went to the University of Virginia and received my MBA from the Wharton School at the University of Pennsylvania. I've just started my own business developing medical computer software."

It was exciting to discover this Sunday school for super-stars and find that they wanted to be a part of the church—even if it made me wonder what I was doing with all my extra time.

One person after another introduced themselves in a sharp, upbeat, confident manner, until we got halfway around the circle. And then:

"Umm. . . . Hi. I'm Don Smith. I graduated from Independence High School in Charlotte. And . . . umm . . . I drive a truck, but I'm out of work right now and . . . umm . . . I'm staying with a friend here until I can find something new."

The room was now still for two long, uncomfortable seconds. We sat silently, painfully aware that something was not right. This Christian gathering was unprepared to reach out to Don with understanding and compassion. So with no further attention to him, the group moved on.

"Hi. I'm Sarah Jones. I graduated from . . ."

I have thought many times over the years about that experience and what was exciting about it and what was wrong with it. All churches reflect the cultures in which they exist. Of course, there is nothing wrong with being a CPA, lawyer, or CEO. And there is nothing wrong with graduating from an elite university. Yet there is something wrong, especially in the church, with making someone feel anything less than a child of God. The problem that morning was that the teachings of Jesus Christ were not embodied in the life and experience of the class. The competition and striving of the dominant American culture were incarnated in that morning's gathering, and no attempt was made to resist the seemingly overwhelming influences of our commercial world.

Churches at the periphery push back against the competitive, market-driven pressures that weigh down on people so heavily. One great gift of the small-church experience is the simplicity of life of its people. Not really by design or intention but rather as a matter of course, the small church has little pretense. Of course this does not mean that individuals will not share the same human tendencies to pride and arrogance. But the white clapboard building, the gravel parking lot, and the handcrafted church sign all signal that as a group of people, these folks are not here to impress anybody. They have gathered again simply to be with one another and to worship God.

There is something compelling about what the small church seems to lack, compared to other groups and organizations. These churches often lack resources: money, updated facilities, and a critical mass of people. Sometimes they lack skilled musicians. Sometimes they lack a pastor. Often they lack comfortable pews and a sound system that actually helps one hear the sermon. Yet what is not here tends to highlight what *is* here. Small-church life strips away many nonessentials of being church. But it is not really a stripping away, because this simplicity is a natural occurrence—not something achieved. The lack becomes the opportunity to put on center stage people caring for one another and the experience of Sunday morning worship.

The people's gathering reveals congruence between the experience of handshakes, hugs, hymns, prayers, and words like "Life does not consist in the abundance of possessions." Sitting on the wooden, straight-backed pew next to the aged saint who suffers from arthritis, we look at a young mother and her newborn and remember that the kingdom can only be received as a child. In this small, simple space with its thirty people, a few souls look out the clear-paned windows to the frozen creek and imagine the possibility that the meek will inherit the earth. The people here have known one another for a lifetime. They remember the grandparents of the teenager who wears his high school football sweatshirt to worship, and they remember that his grandfather played football as well. They know what one another will be doing on Sunday afternoon after worship. Knowing people this way means that it's not a big leap when they hear the psalmist say that God knows the number of hairs on every person's head.

In this small, simple setting the smells, sounds, tastes, and feelings resonate with the simplicity of parables like the mustard seed and upside-down teachings like the first shall be last and the last shall be first. This context naturally connects with the sacred stories of the Scriptures that show God's penchant for small things. God's chosen people are the small, socially insignificant, pilgrim people of Israel and not the mighty empire people to the north and south. God gives little Israel victory over the great kingdom of Egypt. David, the youngest, weakest son of Jesse, defeats the mighty Goliath with faith and five smooth stones. God culls Gideon's army down to a small, rag-tag band; their surprising victory displays God's glory. The Messiah comes from rural, forgotten Nazareth—nothing good could come out of there. Twelve guys from ordinary backgrounds and occupations become Jesus's disciples, who follow him through Galilee and eventually to Jerusalem, the cross, and Easter morning. To put it simply: less can be more. Small numbers, simple settings, and out-of-the-way places resonate with biblical stories that often emphasize the same.

This may sound like I am romanticizing the small church. Isn't this all a harkening back, a longing for a simpler and easier time that really never existed? Let me attest to the truth that small-church life is no ideal, no garden of innocence. The small-church pastor endures innumerable bumps and bruises on the pothole-ridden path of small-church ministry. Small-church people and pastors are no less hypocritical and self-centered than large-church people and pastors. The central importance of people caring for people can quickly turn into a parishioner feeling angry about not being cared for enough. The blessing of lack can turn quickly into the curse of want. The small-church experience keeps one always laboring in the struggle to love and wrestling on the mat of making ends meet.

Yet a natural congruence exists between the small-church experience and the story of Jesus and twelve disciples in a rural Galilean countryside, learning parabolic teaching from the lilies, fig trees, foxes, and hens about the kingdom of God. Quite naturally, the small church sees God in and through the ordinary, small details of human relationships and the created world. The intrinsic gift of the small church is its smallness. That people from outside this context have a hard time saying this indicates how overwhelming the dominant culture's message is: bigger is better, more money and resources mean a better life, financial success is a measure of God's favor.

Let's turn the tables around to see how easy it is to affirm a different intrinsic gift. One of the large church's gifts is that, simply because it is large, it can reach out and touch more people with the gospel of Jesus Christ. One gift of the large church is that it is large. More can be more. Thank goodness. I would feel something was horribly wrong if there were not fellow Christians committed to being evangelists of good news to people everywhere. Church leaders have no problem saying that this is true. The large church reaches more people because more people are likely to gather there, which means that more people will be doing the reaching. The large-church experience embodies something akin to the power of Pentecost, which gathered large crowds of people from vastly different cultures, languages, and experiences and told the story of Jesus.

Likewise the small church has its own natural affinities with the people of faith described in the Scriptures. The organic relational patterns among people in these congregations show hints of the simplicity found in the Beatitudes and the Sermon on the Mount. Here is the inherent strength of small-church life. If one takes the time to look lovingly and carefully at the people gathered here, the upside-down wisdom of Jesus's teaching can be found embodied in this simple yet surprising place.

*It was Saturday at supper time. The smell of onions and garlic from the chicken pasta dish filled the hallways of the little Salem Presbyterian Church.*

*Salem Church had always had an annual harvest meal on Saturday and then an anniversary worship service and lunch on Sunday. Whitfield was a wheat farming community like so many others in rural southeastern Washington. The harvest meal was always an occasion to remember. At times, when the wheat prices were up, it was an opportunity for celebration. And when the prices were down, the meal was a moment to support one another.*

*Everyone still remembers the harvest meal, twenty-some years ago now, when the prices were the highest in memory. A fire had taken out almost all of the Sheffields' crop, yet Mike and Annie Sheffield and their young kids came to the harvest meal that year. The congregation put their arms around the family in the best and most easygoing*

*way they could. Prayers were made on the Sheffields' behalf,
and help and food and company were offered along the way
to let them know that they were going to make it. Now this
year, a couple of decades later, Mike Sheffield was there
for the harvest meal, like always. His wife, Annie, brought
the to-die-for apple pie with the lattice-topped crust. And
the food showed up like it always did. What a feast! There
was always so much food that the last couple of years a few
members started taking the leftovers to the food bank.*

*The numbers around the table were smaller than the
meals from years gone by. So many children had grown
up and moved south and not returned to farm the family
farms. But some people who had moved away came back
for the harvest meal. And everyone looked forward to gathering again and sharing food and conversation.*

*The new, young pastor fresh out of seminary, the
Reverend Peter Striver, stood to offer the blessing. Just as
soon as he said, "Let us pray . . . ," through the open windows came the loud, high-pitched cry of a circular saw.
"What the devil is that?" Darrell Planter exclaimed. The
minister stopped and looked up, saying, "Oh, no, I thought
they knew that we were having the harvest meal today. It
looks like the workers are up on the roof next door."*

*Salem Presbyterian Church and First Baptist Church
were both built in Whitfield in 1895. The churches were
next-door neighbors generation after generation. In 1983
the Baptists bought a larger piece of property on the out-
skirts of town. They moved out there and built a new,
more contemporary building. That same year a newly
formed independent church bought the former First Baptist
building and began the Church of the Holy Spirit. So the
Presbyterians and the Pentecostals have been neighbors*

*ever since; sometimes slightly wary neighbors, but good
neighbors, nonetheless.*

*"Goodness gracious," Darrell Planter said. "What's all
that racket going on next door? Are they over there speaking in tongues and rolling around on the floor again?" To
which Annie Sheffield quickly retorted, "Darrell, behave
yourself. You should learn a thing or two from them." Her
husband, Mike, knew the foreman on the job and was already headed over to speak to him. The construction crew
called it quits when they realized that a social gathering was
going on next door. Annie explained to Darrell that the
Church of the Holy Spirit had decided to finish the steeple
on their building.*

*The Baptists had built a small tower when they put up
the current building in the 1920s. They had left the top of
that tower flat, because the money had started to run out.
They intended to finish off the tower with a nice steeple
sometime in the future. But they just never got around to
it. It looked fine as it was, and there always seemed to be
something more pressing. So the building stayed the same,
until that harvest meal when construction started on the
Church of the Holy Spirit steeple.*

*The next Monday morning Pastor Striver was in his
study and on his third cup of coffee when the phone rang.
Betty, the church secretary, told Pastor Pete that Darrell
Planter would like to talk to him. "Hi there, Pastor. I was
wondering if I could come down to your office and chat
with you awhile this morning." Pete knew that Darrell's
family had been in the Salem Church for generations.
Darrell was the last one of the Planter family to run the
big wheat operation south of Whitfield. Darrell and Sarah's
two grown sons had moved away years ago and attended*

*college in California. Neither one wanted to carry on the family tradition of farming. So when Darrell retired, he sold everything and made a bundle of money. He had donated the funds for the new gymnasium at the high school, which was named after him. So Pete was nervous when Darrell called, because it was not likely that Darrell needed pastoral counseling. More likely was that Darrell had a project in mind.*

*When Darrell arrived, he had two lattes in hand. "Hi there, Pastor. I knew you liked your coffee. Hey, why don't you walk outside with me?" The two of them walked from the office through the solemn, split-chancel sanctuary as the hardwood floors creaked under their feet. Out the front door and across the street, they walked together. And then they turned around, looking back across the silent street at the Salem Church.*

*Pete said, "What are we looking at, Darrell?"*

*"Do you see it, Pastor? Can you imagine that new steeple on the church next door?"*

*Puzzled, Pete said, "Yeah, I guess I can."*

*Undeterred, Darrell continued, "Their new steeple will be taller than ours now."*

*Pete sighed, "Does that bother you?"*

*"Well, of course it bothers me, Pete. I thought surely it would bother you too, being well educated at that Ivy League seminary in New England. How in the world can we let the Pentecostals have a taller steeple than ours? It's not right. The people in this church built most of this town. We can't let the Pentecostals think that they're more important than us. We have to keep up and compete, Pastor, or we'll get left behind. We need to rebuild our church tower and raise our steeple. And I'm ready to pay for it."*

*For the next fifteen minutes Pete and Darrell stood on the sidewalk in front of the two churches arguing for and against entering "the Great Steeple Chase." With each passing moment their faces were becoming redder and their voices were getting louder. Pete realized that he was coming close to saying something that he would regret. So he ended the conversation and hoped and prayed that it would end there, but he stewed about it the rest of the week.*

*The next Sunday Pastor Pete walked to the church to put the final touches on his sermon notes. One by one people drifted into the church building. Jennie was putting on the coffee. Jim and Dee were greeters that morning and took their spot at the door. Frank was frantically running off the bulletins. The choreography of Sunday morning worship had begun once again. The buildup before and the worship itself were like a wonderful dance, like one of the called dances at the Grange Hall. Pete tried to watch and notice each part, but sometimes it's hard to see it all. He did notice Dacia Thompson outside on the sidewalk talking to a little girl.*

*Dacia Thompson was retired from Whitfield Elementary School where she had answered phones and kept school calendars for the better part of three decades. Dacia still enjoyed children of all ages, from toddlers to high schoolers. She had never had any kids herself, and she lamented that there were no children at Salem anymore. But one morning she struck up a conversation with a little five-year-old girl named Emma Jewell. Emma lived across the street from the church, and although she never went to church, she liked to watch the people going in on Sunday morning.*

*Dacia began parking her car on the other side of the street on Sunday, just hoping that Emma might be outside.*

*Dacia had even introduced herself to Emma's mother, because she didn't want to frighten either Emma or her parents. Although Dacia wanted to invite Emma to church, she was hesitant of pushing too hard. She had discovered that Emma's mother was raising Emma on her own, after being divorced. Emma was sad and still grieving that her dad had moved away. She saw him about once a month.*

*So Dacia and Emma talked about pets, about whether dogs were better than cats or vice versa. They talked about their favorite foods, and Emma tried to describe her favorite desserts and candies. They talked about which season of the year was the most fun. Was it the flowers in the spring or jumping in the leaves in the fall? These conversations reminded Dacia that the simple things were so often the most important; the simple gifts were the ones that lasted.*

*That morning in church Pastor Pete preached a well-received sermon on Jesus teaching the disciples about the cross. The people joined voices and sang together with feeling "When I Survey the Wondrous Cross." Later that night the session had its monthly meeting. Pete was surprised to see that Darrell Planter and two other members (all three not on session) had come to the meeting. Darrell wanted time on the agenda to speak. Pete knew what the topic would be, and his anger at not being told before the meeting that Darrell was coming with supporters was evident in his red face. As the tense situation unfolded over the course of the meeting, Darrell and Pete ended up shouting at each other, to the astonishment of all the elders. Darrell argued for adding a new, taller steeple. Pete argued for directing any donation to the local food bank. The two were locked in mortal combat, neither able to hear anything but his own voice.*

Mike Sheffield finally broke the tension and made a motion to table the conversation until the following Sunday so everyone would have a chance to cool off and think further about these matters. The motion carried, and people left in silence.

The next Sunday, a beautiful late-summer morning, the dance was beginning again as people arrived at church. Dacia Thompson had parked her car across from the church. But she did not see Emma outside her house. So she waited awhile, fiddling with her purse and then adjusting the rearview mirror, hoping that Emma would come out her front door. But no luck.

Already in the church, the session had gathered for a called meeting and had been behind closed doors for half an hour. Pastor Pete apologized for his outburst at the previous meeting. He stated that he had already shared what he needed to say and would abide by whatever decision the session would make. Darrell softened with this news and more quietly restated his desire to fund a new steeple. Both Pete and Darrell stepped outside while the session finished their deliberations. The elders voted unanimously to thank Darrell for his continued support for the church and his generosity, but they thought that the existing steeple worked just fine for the Salem Church. So the Great Steeple Chase was over before it had begun, and now people were gathering in the sanctuary for worship.

The church sang together the last stanza of Frederick Faber's hymn, "There's a Wideness in God's Mercy": "If our love were but more simple, we should take God at his word; and our lives would be all sunshine in the sweetness of the Lord." Then Annie Sheffield stood up in her pew, because she was the lay reader that Sunday. When she took *a step into the aisle, a young voice cried out from the back of the sanctuary, "Dacia, are you here?" Everyone turned around to see little five-year-old Emma Jewel standing in the narthex with a shocked look on her face as the whole congregation turned around staring right at her. Dacia motioned with both of her arms for Emma to come and sit down with her. Emma ran down the middle aisle to the third pew on the right and quickly slid in next to Dacia.*

*"I missed you this morning," Emma said. "My mom said it was okay to come over to the church and see if I could find you here. Is that okay?"*

*"Oh, yes," Dacia said. "That is wonderful."*

*Annie smiled as she walked up the chancel steps to the pulpit. She opened the big, black, pulpit Bible and read the Scripture from the eighteenth chapter of the Gospel of Matthew:*

*At that time the disciples came to Jesus and asked, "Who is the greatest in the kingdom of heaven?" He called a child, whom he put among them, and said, "Truly I tell you, unless you change and become like children, you will never enter the kingdom of heaven. Whoever becomes humble like this child is the greatest in the kingdom of heaven. Whoever welcomes one such child in my name welcomes me."*

*"The word of the Lord," Annie said.*

# CHAPTER 3

# *Limits*

*We can do no great things, only small things with great love.*
          Mother Teresa, *Love, A Fruit Always in Season*[1]

*O to grace how great a debtor, daily I'm constrained to be!*
*Let that grace now, like a fetter, bind my wandering heart*
*to Thee.*
          Robert Robinson, "Come, Thou Fount of Every Blessing"

The charms of small-church simplicity appeal to so many small-church folk. They love their churches and will tell you what their congregations have meant to them. This will sound remarkably small church partisan, but the happiest and most fulfilled pastors that I know are small-church pastors who have been at one place in ministry long enough to be adopted into the place and the people. Both pastors and laity feel great satisfaction and love for their small churches. But it is getting harder to find new pastors who will take that initial plunge into a small, peripheral-church context and the cultural transition it so often involves.

My own denomination counted up congregations without pastoral leadership in 2010, and the results were striking but not surprising. Of the 6,865 churches with a membership under 150, 1,814 were congregations without pastoral leadership. Of the 381 churches with a membership over 800, one congregation was without pastoral leadership.[2] The quick explanation for this reality is that small churches do not pay enough to keep their pastors. But this is far from a full exploration of why mainline denominations are having a difficult time generating small-church pastoral leadership. The reality is that the distance between center and peripheral cultures is growing, making communication and understanding increasingly more difficult. To engage these cultural differences, let us imagine a pastor entering the confusing maze of searching for her first church.

Martha is wrestling to discern what God is leading her to do. She is graduating from seminary in the spring. She sent her resume to a number of large programmatic churches for associate pastor positions. She also sent this information to some small congregations. So far the phone calls that she has received requesting interviews have all come from the small congregations.

Martha graduated from one of the better universities in her home state. After college she decided not to pursue her degree interests in biology, although she had opportunities for work. A number of friends and pastors had encouraged her to consider seminary, and she began to feel that God might have something different in store for her than the biology laboratory. She moved away to attend an academically demanding seminary and excelled in her coursework. One of her professors even suggested that she consider further graduate study.

She had been willing to forego the advantages of a stable and well-paid career in the sciences, but now the thought of moving to a small town and serving a little bitty church in the middle of nowhere was not what she had imagined. Was this the best use of her gifts and abilities? Would she be able to afford serving this congregation? Would she meet people her own age? Could she survive living in a fishbowl? And what about the future? Would she be able to move on to a larger church in a larger environment after serving in this setting?

Most mainline Protestant ministers have been formed in university and seminary institutions that have stressed keeping one's options open and maintaining as much individual freedom and mobility as possible. We spend years in the waters of central culture, and then at the end of a master's degree, we are asked to consider going to a small town of two thousand people with barely an option of an attractive restaurant. Many first-time ministers go from a graduate school environment where they enjoy dozens of casual friendships to a small town environment where they experience the high intensity pastoral relationships of people with expectations.

Seminary rewards the most competitive academic students and shapes people to value the achievements conferred for excelling at this competition. So it should be no surprise that most students clamor for the most competitive positions at the most influential churches. This system works for many people. It helps many candidates for ministry share their gifts and talents for the church's benefit and produces many amazing clergy. But it doesn't work well for everyone. Those students who are not competitive enough to win a position in a central-culture setting will likely experience the baffling collision of center-culture and peripheral-culture values.

When preparing to leave school to take on one's first responsibilities as a pastor in a very different culture, a seminary graduate feels confused and anxious. The worry about being cut off and isolated in a narrow environment is the unnamed, fear-provoking obstacle that keeps so many potential candidates for ministry from being willing to consider small-church ministry in rural or small-town settings. The seminarian has been breathing air filled with central-culture values like mobility, change, innovation, professionalism, and achievement. Yet the small churches that are possibilities for service breathe different air. Peripheral-culture values in these small-church settings are almost mirror images of central-culture values. These peripheral-culture values include place, continuity, dependability, personal commitment, and belonging. All these values across the spectrum of both central and peripheral cultures are positive (see values spectrum at the end of the chapter). The simple distinction is that central and peripheral cultures emphasize different values. Quite honestly, serving a small church is a cross-cultural experience that most seminarians need to contemplate. If the candidate were considering a call to serve a church in France, the cultural difference would be obvious. But leaving Princeton Theological Seminary for Paris, Tennessee, is as much a cross-cultural experience as relocating to Paris, France. The tendency for the seminarian or new pastor is to see the absence of central-culture values in the small church rather than the presence of peripheral-culture values.

Usually, lack of money is the stated reason why small churches are not attractive to candidates. Smaller compensation packages are a real and genuine concern. But contrasting values are often the deeper issue, and these are usually not as well understood as financial differences. On the values spectrum, one important difference is between the central-culture value of individual freedom and the peripheral-culture value of community limits. Both are important and necessary values for the well-being of individual and community life. But here I want to take a close look at the importance of limits in the culture of small-church life. This is not a value that I was taught to appreciate in college or seminary, and it took some time to recognize limitation as an important value. It is true that, especially from the outside and at first glance, limits can appear to be a heavy burden. For myself, I have found them to be a surprising blessing. If seminarians or new pastors can understand limits as a positive value, then they may be able to see many more attributes of the small church that their central-culture eyes have not trained them to see.

Once a young pastor who had taken a small congregation in a small town as a stepping stone had reached the three-year mark and was itching desperately to move to a larger church in a big city. He turned to me with exasperation and said, "I can't deal with this narrow, unchanging group of people anymore. Why do you stay?" I was unsure how to help him in the moment, but I could answer the question from my own experience and responded simply by saying, "Love." The small church is the special place that has helped me learn how to love. And over time these loving covenant relationships have helped me see all the amazing cultural opportunities in this place that my dominant-culture eyes had not seen. From enjoying local music and arts and crafts to the joys of fresh, organic produce from farmer friends to the creativity of people who build their own homes to a deeper appreciation and experience of the natural world, these settings have been ripe with opportunities that I had not expected. These places are so big when it comes down to matters of heart and soul. Small-town and rural life is filled with a multitude of cultural opportunities; it's just a different culture.

The truth is that all ministerial settings have their limits. The largest, most urbane posts place restrictions on their ministers. This is because life puts limits on human beings, even as individuals strain to maintain freedom and independence. Love accepts limitation not as a hindrance but as the context for growth and maturity. Love opens us up to becoming our truest selves even as it closes doors on our options. The couple saying their vows covenants to bind themselves to each other and thus not to others. The loving parent willingly accepts the restrictions of being there for her child when she could be somewhere else. The Christian seeking to love God and neighbor hears the commandments and knows that they are fence posts inside which life flourishes and grows.

Limits are an indispensable part of Christian faith. When God revealed himself on Mount Sinai, the revelation began, "I am the Lord your God, who brought you out of the land of Egypt, out of the house of slavery" (Exod. 20:2). Then the liberating God of freedom spoke the limits of this covenant relationship: "Thou shall not . . ." Already some doors were being closed. The purpose of these limitations was to provide a context for flourishing. Pat Miller, Old Testament scholar, describes the context that the Ten Commandments foster, a community he calls "the good neighborhood."[3]

> The Commandments offer an inviting place to live, a locus for human existence that is defined in ways that make the space and existence within its bounds desirable and good. . . . When others speak about the Commandments, they may speak about the Commandments as marking the "boundaries" of life under God, providing "fenceposts" for direction, marking out the "area" of freedom and responsibility, giving much "latitude" in the moral life. The notion

of the "good neighborhood" is a way of claiming such spatial language.[4]

God creates community and sets the limits within which this loving neighborhood nurtures and forms loving human beings.

Of course there is no commandment to enter or stay in the life of a small congregation. The revelatory limits of the Ten Commandments are different from the limits that one experiences amid small-church life. Yet for the person who willingly enters the life of this covenant people, a similar sacred space can be found that is created within the limitations of this community. It's a good neighborhood. Within this space is a surprisingly roomy and generous arena for loving God and loving neighbor and being loved as well. Upon entering this small community one first sees the boundary markers but once within discovers a surprising freedom of space that invites each person to be who he or she is and share what gifts he or she has. Limits can surely be misunderstood as the castle walls within which a person retreats to escape the challenges and joys of living. Or limits can be positively embraced as a context within which a person enters deeply into one's own life, the lives of others, and the life the Holy Spirit brings forth in all creation.

How many of us as recent seminary graduates upon entering the small church simply assumed the limits were castle walls? I did. It took time for me to really see and appreciate the vitality of God's people in my first church, because I was now in a place of smaller scale. It was small, not big. I was now living in peripheral culture, not central culture. The focus of concern in that church was sharply concentrated on the thirty or forty or fifty souls gathered here. After being in a graduate school and considering global issues, new pastors may find this tight focus provincial and self-centered. While the larger culture may have great causes to fight for, those issues will not be the primary concern here unless they relate to the people. If the pastor is a passionate defender of issues of justice, these issues will have to connect immediately to the people who are present right here and now. Folks in small churches have great conviction about justice and equity. They can be moved to great efforts of sacrificial giving for the sake of others who are not a part of their fellowship. But no cause is worth fighting if the cause takes priority over the people and the remembered cloud of witnesses who have spent a lifetime learning to love one another.

Carl Dudley, seminary professor and small church specialist, articulates this limiting and conserving quality in these words:

> The richest resource of most small churches lies in the feelings about members now, and the memories of feelings that they have had in the past. Being in the place evokes responses worth remembering. Preserving those memories is important to the small church. Conserving the relationship between people, place, and happening is the contribution of many small churches to the pilgrimage of church members. Small churches are not against change. They simply feel that conserving the past is a priority.[5]

Dudley insightfully uses the term *conserving* instead of *conservatism*, because this temperament should not be confused with a fixed ideology. Lay leaders of small congregations have learned this conserving way from leaders they have watched and admired who came before them.

The wisdom of conserving the primary place of this people flows from the conviction that God has called them together to love God and quite specifically to love one another. If a valuable educational or stewardship program from the denomination does not serve this purpose, it will be rejected. If a worthy project from the denomination does not relate in some way to this people, it will be ignored. This limiting, tenacious focus is the conserving temperament of the small church.

I have come to respect this conserving practice as clarity of vocation. They understand their calling as a small church, and they will not allow a pastor or a denominational representative to lead them away from that calling. They have learned to push back when their peripheral identity is challenged by leaders with unacknowledged center-culture expectations. Well-meaning pastors seeking good ends have at times sucked small-church lay leaders dry of time and energy for their primary purpose. Sometimes a lay leader challenges a pastor's project out of love for the people. And sometimes challenging the pastor is a matter of sheer obstinacy. The pastor who seeks to love the congregation will enter the difficult work of helping herself and the people figure out which it is: love or obstinacy. It's not always clear.

Stu was one of the first people to help me see that this patient work of discernment was a big part of what I was called to do. I was right out of seminary at the time. I thought that the biggest part of my calling was to grow the church's membership, and I was busy going about it. I bumped into Stu while I was caught up in these pursuits. Fortunately for me, Stu was a quiet, patient elder in the church. He rarely spoke, but he was someone who was intently listened to by the congregation when he did finally say something. Stu was several years past retirement age, but he still ran the grocery store his father had started. He had done well and was respected in town, even though he still drove the rusted-out, white Ford F150 that people loved to joke about.

I had not realized that I had roused the latent Scottish ire of Stu until he arrived at my study one morning. He came to dissuade me from changing the church's lone Bible study of six to eight souls, which met at the horrible time of 3:00 p.m. on Wednesday afternoon. I had all the right reasons for changing to a better time that would accommodate more people. He seemed stubborn and hardheaded in his resistance to change. Before I could bring this up at a session meeting, his daughter called and wanted to start a new Bible study during Sunday school hour for the "young people." At the moment I felt angry at being outmaneuvered, and now I had two Bible studies to go to!

It took a couple of years for me to appreciate the wisdom of what had happened. The "young people's" Bible study took off, and they enjoyed being together. Over time I came to understand the depth of relationships in the other Bible study, which was a community of people who had spent much of their lives together. One day Stu came prepared for studying the good Samaritan parable. He was engaged in an unusually passionate way that afternoon in his questions and conversation about this passage. He was exploring what it means to serve the needs of neighbors.

Later that same night a crowd of people gathered for a town meeting about a proposal to build a new post office. The town had received word from the state that they could receive funds to build a brand new post office. Everyone was excited by the thought of a new building in town. People spoke enthusiastically for the benefits of an attractive new post office and how it might spruce things up a bit.

Then Stu slowly came forward to speak. People were surprised and wondered what he would have to say. The problem that Stu saw with this whole idea was that the state wanted to build the post office almost a mile out of town on the main highway. This strategy had been employed in numerous small towns as a matter of convenience to the postal workers for getting deliverers to their routes. But this strategy also presented a problem for many. Stu saw people walking to the post office when he drove along Main Street on his way to the store. He knew many of these folks personally, and he knew a number of them did not have cars. He liked the idea of a new building, especially because it would be close to his house, but he was concerned that it would force people to walk long distances to receive their mail. The last words of his short speech were a question, "Should we ask our *neighbors* to walk so far for the sake of our convenience?" The crowd was silent. And the post office stayed. Stu showed me that the small church that focuses so much attention on nurturing its own folks is a blessing to its people in order for them to be a blessing to their neighbors.

Mission and outreach grow naturally out of the depth and commitment of these covenant relationships. The small church will preserve and protect these relationships, and where these relationships are nurtured they will touch other people. People hear the sacred stories of Scripture amid the relationships of family and neighbors and respond by reaching out to their community. This dynamic is not unlike Jesus calling Simon Peter, Andrew, James, and John from their fishing boats to follow him. Their discipleship would grow

amid these family and neighborly interrelationships and be
nurtured in Peter's home in Capernaum and around the table
that they shared before they started traveling to other towns.

One Sunday after church Sandy invited me to go with her
to visit the veterans' nursing home. I had recently begun supply preaching at this small, mountain church of approximately forty members. It seemed like a good way to get to know
some church members, and so I rode with Sandy and her
friend Jan. The veterans' home was in very poor repair, and
the men that I met that day were struggling with numerous
physical and emotional illnesses, as well as having little to no
family and no financial resources. But I was amazed to watch
how the veterans greeted us, and later three others from the
church, with such gratitude. It was a family reunion, like so
many small-church gatherings.

Many years ago some friends from the church who had
family in the military started visiting the isolated men of this
veterans' home. This group of friends has grown into a size-
able mission outreach. They visit twice a month, celebrate
birthdays, play bingo, decorate for Christmas and holidays,
and simply build community. One elder leads an informal
worship service and prays for and with them. They have as-
sisted and contributed to funerals for those who have died.
They know all the men by name and are known by name.
The depth and continuity of these long-lasting relationships
of church friends has created community among the veterans. The continuity of these church relationships has helped
the commitment to this ministry endure over many years.

As modern, technologically minded people, we often dis-
dain continuity. We view it as a sign of bored indifference.
Yet we rarely see how the pendulum often swings so far back

the other way. Our Internet-driven, television-altered minds are addicted to changing scenery, changing images, and changing patterns. How strange it is that the rapid movement of Facebook pages and text messages have become numbing comforts in our highly mobile world. If we have to sit still with the same images in front of us, we are afraid that we will fall asleep. If our lives have to be still with the same people and places in front of us, we are afraid that we will die. "Novelty is a new kind of loneliness, . . . the faint surprises of minds incapable of wonder,"[6] writes Wendell Berry.

Covenant love lives with continuity. People have a smaller sphere of options within covenant. Living and ministering in the small-church context means a number of limits and constraints. They can feel like a straightjacket for the person who has not empathized with or embraced the small church's vocation. But these limitations provide the necessary context for the good neighborhood of meaningful and deeply satisfying relationships. Small churches have quite a diverse range of theological and political perspectives, and the individuals within them have even more diverse perspectives. Yet a healthy small church will practice this limiting work of keeping first things first.

At the same time, the small church has a liberating impulse as well. Within the good neighborhood protected by the conserving temperament of its leaders is an organic hospitality that welcomes a wide-ranging diversity of God's children. This natural acceptance, which makes a place and purpose for each individual, is the topic of the next chapter.

## Values Spectrum

| Center Culture, Large-Church Values | Peripheral Culture, Small-Church Values |
| --- | --- |
| Mobility | Place |
| Change | Continuity |
| Innovation | Dependability |
| Individual | Community |
| Numbers, successful events | People, good vibes |
| Planning, organization | Intuition, fellowship |
| Professional competence | Personal commitment |
| Leadership | Discipleship |
| Achieving | Belonging |
| Democratic decisions led by process | Consensus decisions led by authorities |
| Reflection | Behavior |
| Mind-centered | Heart-centered |
| Present with eye to the future | Present informed by the past |
| *Chronos* time | *Kairos* time |
| Spirituality of personal balance | Spirituality of group flow |
| Young families | Intergenerational relationships |
| Complex, interrelated systems | Single-cell system |

# CHAPTER 4

# *Creation*

*The heavens are telling the glory of God;*
*and the firmament proclaims his handiwork.*
*Day to day pours forth speech,*
*and night to night declares knowledge.*
*There is no speech, nor are there words;*
*their voice is not heard;*
*yet their voice goes out through all the earth,*
*and their words to the end of the world.*
*In the heavens he has set a tent for the sun,*
*which comes out like a bridegroom from his wedding*
*    canopy,*
*and like a strong man runs its course with joy.*
*Its rising is from the end of the heavens,*
*and its circuit to the end of them;*
*and nothing is hid from its heat.*

                                        Psalm 19:1–6

*There is no plant in the ground but tells of your beauty, O Christ.*
*There is no creature on the earth*
*There is no life in the sea*
*But proclaims your goodness.*
*There is no bird on the wing*
*There is no star in the sky*
*There is nothing beneath the sun*

*But is full of your blessing.*
*Lighten my understanding of your presence all around, O Christ.*
*Kindle my will to be caring for creation.*

J. Philip Newell, *Celtic Prayers from Iona*[1]

For years I have struggled to understand how the small church could so doggedly resist outside influences and at the same time so graciously accept each unique personality of its people. What is it that makes for such freedom for people to be so much themselves? Small churches comprise such an extraordinary range of characters, dress, jobs, families, incomes, and perspectives. One could say that love is unconditional and accepts people as they are, and of course this would be true. One could say that the small church is a family and we don't get to pick our family members, and of course this would be true as well. In addition, something structural or intrinsic is built into the relational patterns of this people that is akin to the interconnected and diverse patterns of nature.

The importance of this creation connection came to light for me in a savory bowl of bear stew shared with Michael and Charlotte around their handmade, rough-hewn, hickory dinner table. Michael offered a prayer giving thanks to God for friendship, for mountains, and especially for the life of the bear. He had shot the bear we were eating in a hawthorn patch up on top of the mountain. He had been living on this mountain since he had returned from Vietnam.

"Please pardon, Michael," said his wife Charlotte. "When he prays, you never know if it's going to be eighteenth-century Cherokee, twentieth-century U.S. Army, or Presbyterian elder." To which Michael smiled and said, "I hope all three."

I was there spending a year at Michael and Charlotte's small twenty-five-member mountain church to teach him and another elder how to take over the pastoral responsibilities of their church. They could not afford calling a resident pastor, and their location was too remote to attract a part-time pastor from somewhere else. So on behalf of the presbytery, I was there to teach Michael, this original do-it-yourself homesteader, how to pastor a church. I would learn more from this serene, mountain ascetic than he ever learned from me.

Michael had grown up in urban New Jersey and wanted to serve in the army like his dad. After graduation he went straight to the recruiter's office and ended up fighting through the countryside of Vietnam as a Green Beret. A United States Army Special Forces picture of him, taken before his deployment to Southeast Asia, hung in his cabin hallway. He was a clean-shaven, fiery-eyed, pencil-thin teenager, which was quite a contrast with his current Grizzly Adams appearance. He had earned a host of medals for his bravery. He had survived. And he returned home after the war traumatized by the violence and bloodshed he had seen and of which he had been a part. He headed straight for the Appalachian Mountains and had enough family money to purchase thirty-five pristine acres.

Michael pitched a tent and began digging out a foundation from the mountainside and lining it with granite from a nearby creek. He felled the oak, spruce, and poplar with a crosscut saw to create a magnificent mountain palace. He did it all himself. It gave him work and focus. He hunted the same land. Fifteen years went by before he had electricity run up the mountain.

But it was not long until post-traumatic stress disorder (PTSD) began to tear him apart from the inside. After the longest and most difficult year of his life, he finally reached out. He found a counselor in a town that was a seventy-minute drive from his home. He found a small congregation of the same denomination in which he had grown up in New Jersey. He could walk to the church on Sunday morning in about half the time it took to drive to the counselor. As he built a home, he began to build new connections in his life. Michael said that the most restoring connections were those he discovered in the natural environment as he utilized what he found in it to build his home. Many years later he finished a master's degree in counseling and met Charlotte, who was a wild mix of experiences herself. She was part Asheville aristocracy and part Celtic forest sprite. They had been married eighteen years ago in the little mountain church where they were now such a faithful and loving presence.

Today Michael is employed by the county to counsel local returning veterans from Afghanistan and Iraq who suffer from PTSD. He is one of two lay pastors (officially called Commissioned Ruling Elders in the Presbyterian Church, USA) who minister to his vital small church. He is also an outspoken voice for protecting the environment in his rural county. Through a mix of counseling, church friendships, Bible study, and attentiveness to the natural world, he discovered a way to integrate all his life's experiences. Nature had taught him that nothing is wasted. He prayed for God to heal and redeem all the different parts of his amazing life. And it made me grateful to witness how God's healing and redeeming purposes were touching so many others through him.

The small-church people I have witnessed are connected to creation in ways that have been lost in much of the dominant American culture. This connection to creation makes for a natural appreciation of the diverse members within the small church. Living within the natural world and being a part of it teaches us that everything has a place and purpose.

This wise observation about nature is attributed to John Muir: "When we try to pick out anything by itself, we find it hitched to everything else in the Universe."[2] As this is true in creation, it is also true in the healthy small church. Each one of the very different children of God shares a bond with each other that is deeply felt. Children and grandparents, teachers and students, railway workers and bankers all love to sing together, "We are one in the Spirit. We are one in the Lord." This natural, organic unity amid diversity makes the small church resilient and sustainable.

Much of our modern, technological, center-culture world still assumes that dominating nature is the preferable way to live. Since the industrial revolution modern culture has striven to control and live apart from nature, and this way of living has crept into and taken root in the church. The Scriptures show us a different way.

Psalm 19 begins with proclamation. Yet there are no sermons, no human beings uttering words. Creation tells, proclaims, and sings the glory of God. The silent telling of this story is as orderly as the first creation story. Light, day, night, morning, sky, earth, seas, plants, fruit, sun, moon, stars, birds, sea monsters, fish, cattle, every creeping thing that creeps on the ground, human beings—very good! Creation speaks a visual word, telling the wonders of God's handiwork like the church that gathers to proclaim the same.

Often children's first observations about God come from interaction with creation. The power of ocean waves, the sensation of wind rushing through swaying trees, or the grandeur of a snowcapped mountain peak bring forth questions about God. Is God older than that tall tree? Encountering creation triggers a natural human response that turns our thoughts and feelings to God. In the book *Dakota*, Kathleen

Norris tells the story of a shy, little black girl who moves from Louisiana to North Dakota and after observing the western sky says, "The sky is full of blue and full of the mind of God."[3]

When I lived in the Columbia Highlands of Washington State and pastored small churches in the Kettle Crest and Selkirk Mountains, the natural lessons of interconnection were abundant. As I hiked the Kettle Crest and came to the end of a switchback with an open vista across the glacial-wrought valley of the kettle, it dawned on me that creation was a congregation at worship. Ponderosa, larch, and tamarack stretched upward from their pews reaching their tremendous arms to God. The burning sun cooked the high alpine sage, offering up a heavenly aroma of incense. A red-tailed hawk soared above like a choir solo of flight. I heard no voices, no words, no sermons, and "yet their voice [went] out through all the earth, and their words to the end of the world" (Ps. 19:4).

Long before the church came into being, the earth has been offering this kind of worship. God's glory is in this naturally occurring silent word from the Lord. The beginning of Psalm 19 clearly presents a natural revelation of God in creation. The church has sometimes drawn hard lines between Creator and creation, but this emphasis on separation has not served us and our planet well. The deep connections between God and the environment abound. The Scriptures themselves challenge us to rethink our cultural dependence on technology and our modern tendency to dominate nature. Human beings are part of this creation as well, and our salvation is bound up with all creation. As the apostle Paul wrote, "We know that the whole creation has been groaning in labor pains until now; and not only the creation, but we ourselves,

T-2-00770

Condition: Used - Acceptable

T-2-00770

T-2-00770

SKU: T-2-00770

ISBN: 9781566994330

Title: Imagining the Small Church: Celebrating a Simpler Path

Condition: Used - Acceptable

Entered Date: 5/12/2022

who have the first fruits of the Spirit, groan inwardly while we await for adoption, the redemption of our bodies" (Rom. 8:22–23).

One precious gift of peripheral small-church life is a practical and incarnated doctrine of creation. Much small-church culture is deeply infused with natural rhythm and awareness of the created order. Often people in small churches live lives that are in close contact with their natural environment. Many small churches minister among communities whose work includes farming, foresting, or mining. Those who have ministered in farming churches know how harvest season shapes the life of the small rural church. Yet attention to the natural world is not reserved for those who live in rural and country settings. One can find similar creation awareness in some small urban churches that can be expressed in such diverse ways as community gardening or simply the way a congregation pays attention to the human body.

Healthy and vital small-church culture embodies the love and grace of God in down-to-earth ways. Hugging and touching are a crucial part of what happens on Sunday morning. In this culture human touch is a primary means of communicating the love of God. The body is also a focus during conversation and times of sharing prayer concerns. A friend or family member may be prayed for with graphic description of their sickness. Both physical contact and talk of the body reveal the small church's concern with the natural world.

Attention to the cycle of life and death reveals the small church's deep sense of the created order. Great time and energy are given to key moments in the human experience: births, marriages, birthdays, graduations, weddings, anniversaries, and funerals. The small church trusts that life follows a good and natural cycle. There is an important flow, with different stages of movement in the human life cycle. Wendell Berry articulates this ancient ideal as a wheel of life and describes it this way:

> The ancient norm or ideal seems to have been a life in which you perceived your calling, faithfully followed it, and did your work with satisfaction; married, made a home, and raised a family; associated generously with neighbors; ate and drank with pleasure the produce of your local landscape; grew old seeing yourself replaced by your children or younger neighbors, but continuing in old age to be useful; and finally died a good or a holy death surrounded by loved ones.[4]

People in small-church cultures are keenly aware of these movements in life, and much is said about these transitions amid the congregation. Checking in with people about how they are feeling both physically and spiritually is so important. It's not just the pastor who is supposed to do this. Everyone does this. In fact, many meetings are completely given to this kind of checking in. These human experiences are not something other than what church business is about. They are the very stuff of church life. Here, the Christian life is about paying attention to this cycle of life within oneself and learning to live well where one is. Then one must pay attention to where other people are on this cycle and be sensitive to each stage's difficulties. This awareness of the life cycle is at the heart of what it means to love God, neighbor, and self in this context. When people do it well over a long period, they become identified as the saints of a congregation.

This constant attention to the wellness of body and spirit is why intergenerational relationships are so important in the small church. People at different stages in the cycle of life have something to learn or something to remember from others at different stages. Everyone has a place and a purpose. Everyone has something to learn and something to teach.

One line of thinking about small churches is that they have to focus on intergenerational programming because there are so few people. I can't tell you how many times I've heard intergenerational Christian education being talked about as a last-ditch strategy. I guess the thinking is that if a church doesn't have twenty third graders, then it should resort to an intergenerational model. But quite the opposite is true in the small church. Intergenerational learning is the primary strategy. It doesn't happen only in Sunday school. This learning happens in worship, at potluck suppers, during children's messages, and at visits to the retirement home. Small churches are intrinsically intergenerational because of their attention to the full human life cycle. Only a few people are needed for this work to be done well. A small scale of relationships, ample time to communicate across generations, and natural encounters, especially between the elderly and children, are some of the great opportunities for deepening the Christian faith in the small church.

Small-church life is natural or organic life. Center-church-culture programs and long-range planning are not part of the small-church experience. Dominant-church-culture over-building and overconsumption are not part of this experience. Neither are fixation on money and influence. Intrinsic to the small church's very being are, simply, people and places. What is valued most is the holiness or wholeness of the people of God and the sanctity of the place on earth where these folk gather. This organic life reflects the small church's faith that God has made all things well. All that is needed for its life together has already been provided. What already is in place is a gift of God and is enough to prompt the gratitude of the people of God. What freedom this gives to the people of the small church to be who they are, to recognize in themselves and one another their value as children of God at whatever age.

Much of peripheral small-church culture practices an interrelationship with the environment and embodies interconnectedness with creation. People's daily experience of a diverse natural world helps them relate to the diversity of ages and experiences of others in the church. Another person's age or clothes may look very different, but all are part of a whole given its unity by one Creator. The reason for this natural interconnectedness is not because the small church has been studying the latest green technology, nor has it been involved in the national debate about global warming. Some small-church culture strongly resists the environmental movement as a whole. I've witnessed folks who poke fun at Al Gore and his "inconvenient truth telling," but many of these same people live lives that embody interconnection with the natural world that outshines their vocal green counterparts.

While environmentalists may not see the small church as a companion in efforts to build a sustainable and environmentally sound future, maybe they should. And while denominational judicatory leaders have long bemoaned small churches for not being *sustainable* or *viable*, maybe they shouldn't. The reason why small-church life often shares much in common with the sustainability movement is simply because it has never strayed far from the natural world.

*Webster's New World Dictionary* lists these first six defi-
nitions for the entry *sustain*:

> 1. to keep in existence; keep up; maintain or prolong. 2. to
> provide for the support of; to provide sustenance or nour-
> ishment for. 3. to support from or as from below; carry the
> weight or burden of. 4. to strengthen the spirits, courage of;
> comfort; buoy up; encourage. 5. to bear up against; endure;
> withstand. 6. to undergo or suffer.[5]

Small churches are sustainable because they have developed skills for attending to people and places. They have
remained in existence for decades and centuries, providing
spiritual sustenance and nourishment for many. They have
carried many burdens but have managed to strengthen and
encourage generation after generation. They have borne up
against pressures without and within. They have endured
long periods of poor clergy leadership and often no clergy
leadership at all. They have withstood the temptations to
market and sell the church. And being human and part of
the natural world, they have suffered. All this is true because
they have loved people and places.

Another connection that the small church shares with
the sustainability movement is a mindful awareness of eating. Of course eating is something that connects all human
beings to one another. Attention to what we eat and what
is good to eat has been brought to our awareness by those
concerned with the well-being of our environment. Several
prominent writers like Michael Pollan, Barbara Kingsolver,
and Bill McKibben have alerted us to the unhealthy practices of large agribusiness producers of meats and produce.
Local farmers' markets have blossomed in both rural and

urban settings. Many people have changed the way they buy food, with a growing emphasis on buying local and a willingness to slow down and wait for healthier choices. I've seen small churches develop community gardens to provide healthy vegetables for local food banks. One church I served provided space in the fellowship hall for sharing vegetables among the congregation and serving as a source of eggs from parish chickens.

Small-church culture knows how important eating is. Each small church I have served loves to talk on and on about how much they love to eat together. The punch line usually ends with the old joke about the third sacrament being the potluck supper. Among many rural and country church folk, attention to healthy food is nothing new at all. Eating locally is a practice they have exercised all their lives, because their mothers and grandmothers and great grandmothers all planted vegetable gardens. Their fathers and grandfathers and great grandfathers all raised a few cattle for milk and beef. This self-reliance is learned common sense shared from one generation to the next. Yet for many in the small church, it transcends simple commonsense strategies for making ends meet. Cultivating one's own food, growing vegetables, tending fruit trees, and husbanding animals all connect a person to creation and teach what it means to be human.

So it is no stretch of the imaginations of small-church folk to understand food and eating as an exercise of faith. The dining room table is never far from the communion table. In fact, quite often the cup I have enjoyed around the communion table was filled with grape juice from a parishioner's vines and the bread was baked in a parishioner's oven. In this culture it is clearly more healthy to be a scrappy small farmer than an agribusiness farmer and preferable to be a small church than a megachurch. We can see these ancient realities expressed in the sacred stories of Israel's beginnings.

Pharaoh was in the business of warehousing food through mass farming and extensive irrigation.[6] Food was a weapon. The foods and grains that Pharaoh and the overbearing Egyptian empire stored could be useful weapons to force people into slavery to do their will. Through Moses's leadership and during forty years of wandering in the wilderness, Israel learned a different way, and God delivered them to a new kind of life. On the periphery, they learned to trust that the little bit of manna provided each day would be more than enough for them as a people. It was a hard lesson at first. And more than one person longed for the days of slavery when they had more than enough bread from the fleshpots of Egypt. Yet the providence of God turned out to be steadfast and sure. The little bit of manna came, and in time a little bit of land would come to cultivate vineyards and crops. Food was a gift. There was never enough food or land to exercise power and dominion like the great empires to the south and north. Yet there was always enough to be the people of God and to live the life for which they were created. Who would have thought that little, marginal Israel would be more sustainable as a people than the mighty, dominant empire of Egypt?

The organic connections of the small church with the natural world make its people strong and resilient. As an interconnected part of creation, the small church finds its source of life in our Creator. And each wonderful, unique creature of God has a special place and purpose here.

# CHAPTER 5

# *Belonging*

*The sure provisions of my God attend me all my days;*
*O may Your House be my abode, and all my work be praise.*
*There would I find a settled rest, while others go and come;*
*No more a stranger, or a guest, but like a child at home.*
Isaac Watts, "My Shepherd Will Supply My Need"

*All our reasoning reduces itself to yielding to feeling.*
Blaise Pascal, French mathematician and philosopher[1]

The numerical height of mainline Protestantism in the United States occurred in the year 1965.[2] That was the year that the largest percentages of American people affiliated with and attended church. More Americans were going to church than at any other time in U.S. history. Where I live in the South, this "highpoint" is usually considered to have occurred several years later. The highpoint was the late 1960s, not 1776, when our nation was being born through a bloody rebellion against England, nor was it 1861, when our nation began the brutal internal struggle of the Civil War and saw the beginning of the end of slavery. Nineteen sixty-five was the year *The Sound of Music* premiered in New York City, the year that 3,500 U.S. Marines arrived in South Vietnam, the year that President Lyndon B. Johnson signed the Social Security Act, establishing Medicare and Medicaid. Nineteen sixty-five was the year that CBS first aired *A Charlie Brown Christmas*. In other words, it wasn't that long ago. In the living memory of many church people are the days when we were most popular in our nation's history.

We tend to get nostalgic when thinking back on the church's role in American society. We have let our frustration with our fairly new status as the peripheral mainline of Protestantism today create a festering illusion in our minds. The change in our social location from being at the center of culture to moving toward the periphery has clouded our vision. We dream that once upon a time all our churches were big, bustling centers of activity, filled with children, distinguished by selfless service to the community, and immersed in happy, loving relationships between people.

Yet consider the reality of what churches actually looked like in this era. Less than a decade after the apex of American church growth, the Presbyterian Church in the United States (the former denomination of Presbyterians in the southern states) published the work of a task force reporting on the small church. By 1974 when this report was published, the southern Presbyterian Church was near its numerical height. The church was booming. So our nostalgic memories should be chastened by the reminder that in 1974, 73 percent of these churches had a membership of fewer than 250 members. And 44 percent of these churches had a membership of under 100 members![3] So the truth is that even during the "glory days" the majority of our churches were small.

As mainline Protestants, we are still working through our fixation with numerical decline. We used to be the popular kid in class, but now—not so much. One response to this changing circumstance has been the creation of an unrealistic mental picture: once we were a great and glorious church, but now we are doomed to the dustbin of history. This fanciful delusion keeps us from seeing the ministry right in front of us. This Camelot-like dream diverts us from both the joys and the challenges of being the church today. We have romanticized our triumphs. We have confused our former popularity and status in the culture with being the church of Jesus Christ. We pine for the glories of our misremembered past.

So today, as we evaluate the church through relentless, overbearing market analysis, we mistakenly use dominant-culture tools to understand our present situation. We have less power, less money, and fewer numbers. So we think we must be dying, because life can only be measured by numbers and money. Right? Ironically, the proof of our decline is not lessening power, money, and influence but rather our commercialized, dominant-culture idolization of the market. We see our situation through the same spectacles that the dominant, secular American culture views the world. The problem is not that we are getting smaller and more peripheral. The problem is a lethargic faith imagination and a graceless covenant love.

Small churches, especially small rural and neighborhood urban churches, have an advantage in this changing context. They are less likely to be stuck in the unrealistic, pining daydream about past power and prestige. These churches did not feast on the popularity boom of the fifties and sixties. Here, one will not see reminders of the glory days; no sanctuary that will seat five hundred; no pictures of hallowed ministers from yesteryear; no monuments to influence and position.

Small, peripheral-church folk may bemoan the waning influence of Christianity on American culture. But this is a different kind of lament. And after the last decade's shameless greed and endless military campaigns, they have good reason to bemoan the loss of Christian influence. The small-church lament is not about being left behind. It was always behind, always out of step, and always at the margin. The small-church lament is that things are not as they should be. And that lament has a long, important tradition in the life of covenant people. Angry protestations about declining membership rolls and budgets do not offer a prophetic word to the church. But paying closer attention to people and places and speaking out about who people are and what they are created for carry the potential for genuine transformation.

Healthy, vital, peripheral churches continue to tell and, more importantly, show people that they belong to God. In many different contexts, through many different styles of worship, with many different theological perspectives, the small church embodies the truth that human beings belong to God. In my own denomination, we have spoken throughout our confessional history about belonging to God. Since the time of John Calvin, the language of belonging to God has been part of the Reformed tradition's faith vocabulary. Consider the opening question and answer in the Heidelberg Catechism:

> *What is your only comfort, in life and in death?*
> *That I belong—body and soul, in life and in death—not*
> *to myself but to my faithful Savior, Jesus Christ.*[4]

I remember hearing a wonderful saint of the church, at her congregation's 150th anniversary, give witness to what her church had meant to her. And I can still hear Martha saying, "These are the people who have helped me learn that I *belong* to God." When I talked to her a few days after her speech, she said that she was unaware of the confessional and theological history of *belonging* to God. She wasn't quoting the confessions. She was simply describing from her heart the faith that she had learned through the meaningful relationships with family and friends of the church. My hunch is that she had learned this particular language of faith from the pulpit and from Sunday school. But what sunk that abstract theological learning deep within her soul was the depth of feeling and love she had experienced with others. While I find the language of the confessions beautiful and sustaining, they matter most when they are incarnated in the congregation's life.

Feeling is the heart and soul of small-church life. Small-church folk experience Sunday morning through a combination of feeling, memory, and intuition. This openness to feeling gives people a deep and tenacious sense of belonging, both to one another and to God. These feelings that build up over years spent together make for a depth of commitment and a willingness to give generously of oneself for the church. Feelings of love and acceptance, feelings of empathy and compassion are powerful motivating forces for good that sustain people over a lifetime. People's openness to feeling and attention to human emotion help to embody in church life abstract concepts like belonging to God. Human beings depend on more than head knowledge to trust that in life and in death we belong to God. The feelings of warmth and acceptance, the demonstrations of hugs and visits, the space for tears and anguish, the visible smiles and laughter allow for the whole of a human being to know that he or she belongs to God.

The most important question I carry around throughout the week is this: "How are you feeling today?" This question is a never-fail conversation starter. It may elicit a response about how someone is actually feeling. Or it may bring on a description of what has happened during the week. But I've never seen anyone hesitate in responding to it. Sometimes I slip back into a more familiar question from my own background and experience. "How are you doing today?" This question sometimes creates a hesitation for small-church and rural folks. My sense is that it makes them process their sense of well-being in a way that is secondary to them. Feeling and intuition is their primary way of processing how they are doing. And after watching this now for a number of years, I think there is something to be said for it.

As much appreciation as I have for being in touch with one's feelings, the truth is that I process most of life through my head. I have spent much of my life being taught and trained to do so. I see great value in theological reflection and thoughtful discernment. But they do not guarantee well-being. Small-church life has taught me to be more open and attentive to my feelings. Even more so, I have discovered that attending to persistent emotions can be a trustworthy guide. This is not an argument that emotion is more important than reason. My learning from small-church life is simply that the whole human person is important: heart, soul, will, and mind. This experience has made me more sensitive to how overly head-oriented central culture is. The small-church cultures in which I have ministered tend to be overly heart-oriented, and I have spent much time encouraging small churches to use their heads as well as their hearts. Yet I am grateful for their way of being, which reminds me that integrating the whole of who we are is important.

One of my hopes and prayers is that the denominational church structures might attend more to the feelings that underlie our ongoing discussions about where mainline

Protestantism is going. Underneath the rational arguments and statistics about mainline decline is great pain and loss. Disbelief, anger, and sadness are some of the feelings that have not been attended to in our social transition from popularity to the sidelines. In a head-dominated world it's hard to come to grips with these feelings. Yet until we work through the loss of our former standing in the culture, we will not be able to accept that the Holy Spirit is still at work and still calling us to participate.

What is even more difficult for us is where dealing with these emotions might lead us. Confusion, anger, and grieving point to the painful reality that much of our sense of belonging was placed in the popular social status and influence we used to enjoy. While our confession of faith states that we belong to God, what was actually going on when we spoke the words was sometimes very different. Our anguish is an indication that we often feel our deepest sense of belonging in a cultural position of centrality. And this is a difficult realization to come to grips with. We are now challenged to think and act in different ways. The small church offers us one option among others in this new situation. Here in this peripheral setting we see that belonging to God is given flesh in relationships with others.

Pam and John were refugees from the plummeting real estate market of the urban West Coast. As realtors in Los Angeles, they had prospered during the boom, but they were looking for a place to land during the bust. They had friends with land in our rural little piece of the world and parked their RV in the woods of the Selkirk foothills. Their two children and their task of building a new house focused their attention. But they were not accustomed to being alone in the wilderness. Feeling beaten up and worn out, one Sunday they warily poked their heads into church. At first small-church hospitality seemed a little overwhelming. So they disappeared for a month. Later they reappeared and genuinely appreciated the warm greetings and the shared vegetables and fruit. John came to the Mangy Moose restaurant for the men's breakfast one Friday morning and found new friends. When a few of the men showed up at his place on Saturday to help him work on his new property, he was surprised when nothing was asked in return.

One afternoon Pam and John set out camping chairs on their property and the three of us sat outside enjoying the beauty of the tamaracks, aspen, and mountains. They shared the story of their move, and I realized that not only had they been beaten up by the economy but also by the independent megachurch that they had left behind. They were on a faith journey. They were building a new life, and they wanted a life that had room and space for God and other people. In their previous church experience, they had been quizzed on their theology and prodded about their financial giving. Now people were asking about how their kids were getting along in a new school and whether it was okay for a neighbor to bring over his tractor to level out John's gravel driveway.

Pam said that the first Sunday she had noticed a sign on the church bulletin board that said, "No matter who you are or where you are on life's journey, you are welcome here." She confessed that she had laughed to herself when she had read it. Then clearing her throat so as not to show her emotion, she said that she had never really experienced that kind of welcome before. She was deeply grateful for the hospitality that they had received. But she wondered if another shoe was about to drop. Was there still a religious litmus test to be passed? What would be expected of them? I encouraged them to take their time and find out for themselves if the welcome was genuine. As for expectations, I said that the church would be a place that would encourage and challenge them to love God and to love neighbors and themselves.

Over the next three years they found a place of genuine belonging in the church and in the community. Folks noticed the weight that seemed to lift from their shoulders. They found creative ways to share the tremendous personal gifts that God had lavished on them. Pam sang in the choir and started a choir for the children; she also joined the community theater group and volunteered at the school. John became a part of the Mangy Moose men's group, played his guitar in worship from time to time, and invited people to his newly built house to gaze at the stars through his powerful telescopes. The youth became interested in learning the constellations so that they could identify for themselves what was in the night sky.

When my family and I left and moved back east to the Appalachian Mountains, Pam was on the search committee for the new pastor. Even before we were gone, she was talking about finding a minister who would appreciate and work well with the most important gift of this little church: hospitality.

Belonging and hospitality are two sides of the same coin. Finding a place to belong is the receiving side of this gift of grace. Welcoming a new face is the giving side of this same gift. The love of Jesus Christ is felt deeply in both receiving and giving this grace. Healthy churches of all sizes participate in this grace. Unhealthy small churches make it difficult to be a part of the community and fail to extend hospitality to newcomers. Yet the healthy small church that is open to these gifts has a unique advantage in that the newcomer can be a part of the whole. In this small, intimate community, it is possible to know and be known by each member of the body of Christ. Over time this intimacy creates strong attachments and deep commitments that make the small church strong and tenacious. In a season when the mainline church is losing many of the old cultural props, feelings of belonging and gifts of hospitality may be the small church's greatest gifts.

One of the most emotional experiences I have had in the pastorate was with a friend named Buck. Buck was determined to share hospitality with me during the last year of his life, his sixtieth, the only year of his life that I knew him. He wanted me around as he was succumbing to a melanoma skin cancer that had spread to his pelvis, liver, and brain. He was an independent western soul. He built his two-story A-frame home himself with timber from a relative's lumberyard. And he would have died no other way than in this place, even if that meant less access to modern comforts. He shared the last part of his journey with family, friends, and neighbors as people came and went from his home.

His long, white beard and the fiery red and orange Harley-Davidson shirt reminded everyone what a passionate character he was. Around the rugged knotty-pine family table, Buck entertained friends and family with tales of travels to different parts of the world where he and his wife had lived before coming home to Ferry County, Washington. He relished telling wild tales of racing cars and motorcycles on the dirt tracks of this mountain community. But what he really wanted to tell was his own faith story.

The part of the story that the whole church knew was how years before he had wanted to come to the church where his wife had grown up. But he worried about whether he would be welcome to show up in church. He worried about whether he was acceptable enough to go. He worried about whether his presence would be an embarrassment to the memory of his wife's parents and grandparents, who had been long-time pillars of the church.

When folks in the congregation heard that Buck wanted to attend worship, they went out of their way to let him know how happy they would be to have him there. So he started to come. Later he eventually got involved in an AA support group. The church's acceptance and welcome was a life-changing experience for Buck. It was the most important experience for him in his rekindled faith and his understanding of God. Over the years Buck became involved as a church leader and was ordained as an elder. He became a one-man hospitality crew, sitting on the back pew in his little mountain church. He made sure any new face received a warm and genuine welcome. You could count on any child in the church being greeted and made to feel special by Buck. He felt a deep sense of belonging among this people, and he wanted everyone to be able to share this experience.

I had seen that part of Buck's life each Sunday, and then I saw more when I conducted his funeral, the wildest ride of a funeral I have ever experienced. I know that in my lifetime I will never again see so much leather in a church. When I went into the sanctuary an hour before the service, I saw the coffin on the chancel, painted jet black with red, yellow, and orange Harley-Davidson flames running down the sides. Buck was buried in the shirt with the same flaming colors, the shirt he liked to wear on Pentecost. The crowd filled the sanctuary and spilled over into the fellowship hall where chairs had been placed. Friends were standing in the kitchen and outside the church listening through open windows. The enormous crowd was made up of many folks who were clearly out of their element in a church sanctuary. After the service we lined up in the procession leading to the cemetery, which was led by ten Harley-Davidson motorcycles and five stock cars.

At the graveside I shouted a request for the Stevie Ray Vaughan music to be turned off so that we could proceed with the committal. Then people started again to share their stories about Buck and remember and give thanks to God. He had been the person who had embraced them and spoke of God's love for them. That afternoon I experienced the wild hospitality and welcome of the kingdom in ways I will never forget and cannot adequately describe.

Afterwards, when I started to head home, I took the ferry route across Lake Roosevelt. The lonely lake was empty that day, and only I and one other traveler were on the ferry. It turned out that he was a biker who had been at the funeral as well. He noticed me as the minister who had conducted the service. When he came up to me in his black leather jacket and pants, he was already teary-eyed. Together we enjoyed the quiet, breezy ride across the lake. He struggled to tell me about how Buck had befriended him and saved his life by helping him get into recovery and out of the grip of drugs and alcohol. He described how this experience had restored a faith that had been absent since his childhood. Then he concluded by saying that he and I might live in different worlds but that we both *belonged* to the same God. "Amen, brother" was the only thing to say, as we shook hands and then awkwardly hugged and watched the lake roll by until we arrived on the other side.

In the coming years and decades as the mainline church wanders through a new wilderness, it is impossible to know what lies ahead. Yet the love and resiliency that I have witnessed in these small communities of faith convinces me that they will continue to persevere. Their ability to attend to the whole person—heart, soul, will, and mind—makes them resilient. They will continue to pass on the good news of Christian faith through the intimate, feeling relationships that congregants share with one another and the hospitality they share with neighbors and strangers. The life of these small churches reminds us all that we belong to the God of Jesus Christ.

# Chapter 6

# *Bills*

*My object in living is to unite*
*My avocation and my vocation*
*As my two eyes make one in sight.*
*Only where love and need are one,*
*And work is play for mortal stakes,*
*Is the deed ever really done*
*For Heaven and the future's sakes.*

Robert Frost, "Two Tramps in Mudtime"[1]

I believe that many pastors would find small-church ministry extremely rewarding and meaningful. But the unquestioned reason that so many pastors are unwilling to give small-church ministry consideration is the idea that such churches do not have enough money to support them and their families. Rarely are the assumptions inherent in this conclusion ever brought to light. That's just the way it is. Or at least that is just the way it is in the central-culture ethos from which most seminary graduates come.

The waters of a small town or rural countryside can look very different to those who have been used to swimming at the YMCA or an in-ground backyard pool. Imagine an August trail through the mountains that winds its way to a lush waterfall at the bottom of which gathers a pool of cool mountain water. After shedding a boot and sock, one hiker finds that the water feels cold and threatening to his hot, tired skin. The falling water, the clear pool, and the moss-covered granite and shale are a beautiful sight. The other hiker tosses his boots, socks, and shirt and dives in to discover that the bracing and restoring waters are the best part of the hike. All that he can do to help his trail partner jump in and fully enjoy the experience is to describe it. So let me describe how I got in the waters, left them, and got back in again.

When my wife, Amy, and I were graduating from Union Theological Seminary in Virginia, I was searching for a congregation and Amy was beginning a PhD program. We took out a map and drew a circle with a three-hour perimeter around the university where she would be studying. Our plan was for me to find a church within this circle. I was deciding between a call as the associate pastor of a suburban church or the pastor of a small mill-town church farther away. After prayerful consideration and the wise counsel of a friend and teacher at the seminary, who asked, "Which one of these calls really moves you?" I chose the small mill-town church. That question would stick in my mind as one of several important questions for discerning a call. Amy found a tiny apartment in the home of a family who lived not far from the school. Our little town was a two-hour-and-forty-minute drive for her. It was on the very edge of our circle. We were on the periphery. Amy spent four days a week parsing Hebrew verbs and learning Ugaritic, Akkadian, Ethiopic, and other dead languages remembered by few. Then she would hop in her little Dodge Colt and drive I-85 to spend three days a week in our little town and in the house the church provided, what Presbyterians call a manse.

We loved it! I relished day-to-day life in this little church of loving and faithful people. Visiting and drinking tea on

the porches of parishioners, praying with the elderly, organiz-
ing youth group meetings, studying the Scriptures, preaching
sermons, leading worship, the wild ride of children's messages, moderating session meetings, and the privilege of being
invited into people's interior and prayerful lives; what great
work. At the same time Amy was enjoying her colleagues
and friends and the studying that she was pursuing. This
time confirmed the paths we had chosen, and we entered into
them with great passion and love.

But before long I gave into the temptation that plagues
most ministers. I started watching minister friends and colleagues who were moving up the career ladder. My gaze went
from being engaged in the life right in front of me to turning
sideways to sneak a peek at what others were doing. I found
it amazing how prayer and discernment of a call always led
pastors to bigger churches with bigger compensation packages in more alluring places. I thought back to a conversation at
the presbytery meeting where I was examined for my call to
this little church. During lunch the pastor of a large church in
the big city in the presbytery came up to me and asked, "Are
the two of you going to be able to live on what that church is
paying you?" I was surprised at the question, because after
seminary it seemed like a lot of money, and to be honest,
I hadn't done much comparison shopping. The church provided a manse and paid the annual presbytery minimum salary of $16,500, plus the medical plan and pension. They also
gave us numerous perks: a computer for use at home, fresh-
grown produce, casseroles, and a Christmas check delivered
by Santa himself!

But now I knew what other ministers were making. I had
visited the homes that clergy friends had purchased. I also
saw what my friends from college were making who were in

other lines of work. Truth be told, I began to feel like I was owed more. I was perhaps too anxious or too conflicted to say it aloud, but these were the concerns that began to take root in my thoughts. They were a slow-working poison that sickened my sense of calling.

I wish that I could go back to my twenty-nine-year-old self and say, "Think differently, think creatively about your situation. Consider different ways to provide what is needed for building a family in order to do what you love. This path will be better for your family and for you." But when the news came that we were expecting our first child, I took for granted the common wisdom that was and is like the air we breathe. I looked for a job that paid more. And moving up the ladder was easy. Overnight, it multiplied our income. And I and everyone around me said that it was a calling.

We went to a big Midwestern city and moved into a large, attractive Tudor house in an old, affluent neighborhood. The church had an impressive history of parishioners who were pillars of the city, and the church was wealthy enough that money was not an issue for doing what we wanted to do. People treated us well. They respected my ministry and sought ways to support their church financially. But I discovered that the nature of ministry in this context was very different.

Here, I was a professional minister. Much of my time was spent in preparing what I hoped were impressive sermons that stimulated the educational levels of parishioners. As the church professional, I was responsible for managing the direction of committees and resourcing leaders who prepared a variety of events. Most often moderating the session meant managing conflicts about how the large endowment would be used. I also spent a great deal of time working on our neighborhood business-development council. And much of my energy was spent trying to attract young families in the neighborhood to the church in order to boost the rolls. Much of this work was interesting and provided a new challenge. In most ways it was good and important work. But it was not a calling that moved me deeply.

After several years I began to get nagging, persistent headaches and then lower back trouble. Visits to the doctor proved that the source of the pain was not physical—no disc or skeletal problems, no tumors. It became clear to me that the source was my own tension and dis-ease with a life whose energy, intelligence, imagination, and love were ebbing away. I embarked on several unsuccessful attempts to reconstruct how I went about pastoring the church. People were mostly kind and supportive of their minister, but our hearts were in very different places. What they wanted was a professional minister who would manage the church and grow the membership. My need to be successful and to be liked made it difficult to admit that a change needed to happen. I had promised the pastoral search committee eight years, but after a little over six years it was time to say good-bye.

Amy and I pondered this change together, and we came upon the idea that what was needed was not a new job. What we really needed to do was reorder our lives. By simplifying and prioritizing our family economy, we have been able to do what we love, and I have been able to return and stay in small-church ministry. Now I realize as I look back that we made a deliberate decision to live on the periphery. We still have a foot in center culture as well, in Amy's academic world and in working with larger church structures in our beloved Presbyterian family. But we inhabit a new place, both geographically and spiritually, and this place has provided a new opportunity to creatively craft the lives we love. We have been engaged in this exciting and often challenging effort ever since. In our own experiences of success and failure on this new path, I have come to know in my heart and my gut, and not just my mind, that my primary calling is not to be a pastor. My first and foremost calling is to follow Jesus Christ.

This central Christian calling is what shapes the multiple callings that are unique to me as a child of God. I am a husband, a father, a son, a brother, a neighbor, a lover of nature, a presbyter, and yes, I am a small-church pastor. These specific callings to who I am created to be find their motivation in my primary calling to be a Christian. As a pastor it has been easy for me to confuse my calling to be a minister of Word and Sacrament with my prior calling to follow Jesus.

Our primary Christian commitment challenges us to examine the other multiple commitments of our lives. Christians have done this throughout the ages. One area that Christians have often adapted and creatively adjusted with changing circumstances is the ordering of their family economies. In her book *Tribal Church,* Carol Howard Merritt, pastor and writer, courageously and insightfully tells the story of how young families in her church are coping with a rapidly changing economic environment.

> As congregations reach out to include younger adults in their spiritual communities, they do well to understand that younger generations find themselves struggling in an enormous economic crisis not of their own making. . . . After attending good colleges and working hard every day, young families struggle under tremendous educational debt and jumbo mortgages. With two necessary incomes supporting families it only takes an unexpected illness, a child who

needs additional care, or a layoff to shatter the delicate economic foundation supporting young households.[2]

By describing in detail the hidden stories of struggling urban, professional couples, Merritt brings to the church's attention the difficult economic reality that young families are facing. The drastic economic changes occurring in American culture are putting enormous pressure on different populations, including the young. Merritt rightly presses the older generation of the church to muster more sympathy for these young families and also to be part of the solution by helping them to gain stability in the professional middle class. This willingness to speak honestly and courageously about changing economic pressures is needed in the church. Raising these kinds of questions is natural work for those who are reading the Gospels and attending to the teachings of Jesus.

What I would add to Merritt's discussion is that staying and fighting for stability in the central professional class is only one of many options. I have witnessed numerous young families who have left behind their high-pressured careers that kept them moving every three or four years. Many have sold their high-mortgage homes and taken their kids out of the private elementary schools that charged tuition at the rate of a university. Some have moved back to their hometowns and used their experience to start a business of their own or commute to work in a nearby city. Some have moved to a small-town setting not where they grew up, but an environment they feel is a healthier and happier place to live and raise their children. This kind of simplifying provides the stability that these couples were looking for in the first place. For many of these folks the exodus from the confines of corporate climbing has been nothing short of liberation.

These young families often find that the depth of stable relationships becomes the unexpected source of satisfaction that
makes the change the most rewarding.

Often the church becomes the place where they build
meaningful relationships with people who have lived in these
smaller places their whole lives. And I have watched the older
generation adopt these new families and make them a part of
the church as well as a part of the town or rural community.
It takes economic and vocational creativity for these young
couples to make the change. But they have found that following a job and climbing the ladder is not the only option.
Choosing a small place and then adapting one's work and
career is another way to go.

It is common for pastors to follow a job and then to order
our lives around that job. We live in an ever more market-
driven culture. That families follow jobs is a dominant cultural assumption. Even in the church, our parishioners give
us permission and often congratulations to follow a more
lucrative position, because it will be "better for the family."
That the move will be "better for the family" is simply a
polite way of saying that more money is involved. I'm not
so sure that this is better for families or children, because it
reinforces the assumption that life is more abundant where
things are bigger, entertainment options are greater, and the
money is better. My own experience tells me that this is not
necessarily so.

Getting into the waters of small-church life requires shedding some clothes that are familiar to center-culture life. It
can feel threatening at first for those accustomed to a different context. A different way of thinking and being, especially
about finances, comes with the joy of these waters.

One ongoing challenge for small-church pastors and families is the reality of paying bills. When I began my first call, the trick was simply trying to figure out how to make do with what we had. That was before our kids arrived. My attitude toward this challenge, however, has slowly changed over time. A rewarding part of our Christian life is ordering our lives around our calling by simplifying and letting go of what is not central to who we are and what we do. We have found that there is always enough, even if not as much as would make things easily comfortable. The stretching has made us more engaged in the daily gifts and responsibilities of everyday life.

The creativity of rural-culture people in constructing family economies has been one significant influence on my change in perspective. People here are employed in a variety of work environments. Some of these work environments we might describe as professional and some as working class. Yet in both environments a much smaller percentage of people will follow a job around the country than those in the center-culture professional class. Their priorities usually rank family, friends, and place ahead of job advancement. They will quickly sacrifice quantity of income for quality of life. They exercise great creativity in learning very different kinds of work. They will add part-time jobs from time to time if they like their first job and do not want to leave but need extra income for maintaining their home or sending their kids to college. I am not talking about the working poor who work several jobs and are never able to get their heads above water. The country churches I have served demonstrate great concern for the working poor, and most of our mission energy and resources go to these hard-working folks. The ways that small-church families take hold of their lives and creatively construct family economies have changed how my family constructs our own.

But now let me turn from my own experience and start to meddle a little bit. The reason for my meddling is that in my denomination the call system has become a deterrent to helping many small churches find and especially retain pastors. I apologize in advance for getting so specific with this critique of my own denomination. Most mainline denominations have similar problems with their call systems as they relate to small churches. I hope that my critique will help you reflect on your own denomination's call system and what its strengths and weaknesses are. Our failures stem from the differences between center-culture values and peripheral-culture values and the overbearing dominance of unacknowledged central values in this system. In the Presbyterian Church (USA) we currently use a monolithic system of call that takes a free-market business approach to match pastors with congregations. This system is not working for many of our churches, especially the small ones. Central-culture values of professional skills, competitive compensation, and mobility dominate the current call system. Peripheral-culture values like personal commitment, relationships, and place are not highlighted in this market search process.

Many small churches make this search process work for them despite the fact that it does not fit them well. But what also happens is that many small churches and small-church pastors opt out of the process. It doesn't work for them. Small churches and pastors often find each other through local networks of personal relationships within their judicatory or outside it. But the matches made through these means are relegated to second-class status. These matches are designated *temporary supply* or *stated supply*, emphasizing that they are temporary and not permanent. These matches do not merit presbytery involvement in installation services that build covenant relationships between churches and denominational judicatories. This two-tiered reality only further emphasizes the message from central-culture church to peripheral-culture church: "You are not measuring up. You aren't doing it right." The small church finds this message ironic, because they have often provided the worship and pastoral leadership themselves for months or years when they have not been able to find a pastoral match through the denominational system. Many central churches could not manage this level of lay leadership commitment and skill.

No denomination or other Christian body has a perfect, formalized call system. As long as human beings are involved, we will often stumble and fumble along. The church does experience, however, a great many successes and moments of celebration of callings that exhibit the kingdom of God and embody the ways of Jesus Christ. But the place where we most often stumble is in relationship to our small congregations that cannot afford full-time compensation packages. We have no biblical precedent or theological reason for viewing these congregations as lesser brothers and sisters because their size and resources do not meet minimum salary requirements for calling a full-time pastor. In practice, however, our call system communicates very clearly that there are important congregations and there are less important congregations.

Many small churches, especially those in the range of 100 to 150 members, will be able to continue paying minimum salary packages. If these churches are pastored with small-church wisdom and compassion, many of them will replenish and persevere at a membership level that can support a full compensation package for the pastor. But other churches will not, and denominational leaders need to encourage creative ways for pastoral leadership to flourish in these settings.

I would not suggest scrapping current call systems. They work well for large, programmatic churches. So keep the professional, central-culture search process for the congregations that are programmatic and center culture. We simply need greater variety for different types of churches in different types of cultures. It would be better to allow full citizenship for the small churches and pastors who find each other through local, informal, and interpersonal networks. Denominational leaders should be encouraging and recognizing these positions as permanent pastorates and not temporary pastorates. Denominational leaders should encourage covenant relationships of small churches with denominational judicatories through installation services that involve these congregations with other people from partner churches. This change would help judicatories catch up with what is already happening at the grass-roots level.

The ways that churches and pastoral leadership are finding each other and learning how to creatively construct a relationship are growing exponentially right now. These local, informal strategies will continue to become more important as mainline churches lose resources and power. Like it or not, this is one wave of the future. Pastoral leadership is adapting in these smaller settings in a variety of ways.

*Cooperative ministry* is the new name for the old idea of relating numerous small churches in order to share resources to provide pastoral ministry. More flexibility in those relationships is now being practiced through parish clustering and twinning models. Pressure from on high for congregations to merge or yoke together is a recipe for disaster. But locally led clustering or teaming sometimes proves to be a fruitful experience. Retired pastors and seminary students often serve small congregations. One of the most helpful new adjustments has been the Commissioned Ruling Elder, which took my denomination many years to finally implement. The Commissioned Ruling Elder initiative provides a form of lay ministry. A growing number of trailing clergy spouses have also become a source of pastoral leadership.

Bivocational ministers are another important pastoral leadership option for small churches. Bivocational ministry is growing rapidly, especially in denominations that allow the most freedom at the congregational level. This is not a new model for my own denomination but a return to the older idea of tent making. I have known Presbyterian pastors who were school and prison administrators who have provided long-term pastorates to small churches. I have known UCC and Baptist pastors in long pastorates who have been high school football coaches, mayors, theater directors, home improvement contractors, counselors, children's book authors, and brand managers for Procter & Gamble.

These innovations are really not that new but are a return to the local creativity employed earlier in our nation's history. In the one-hundred-year ministry of the rural church I serve now, only one pastor has had a tenure longer than six years. Most often this church was a pastor's stepping stone to a bigger church. Yet Marvin Williams served for twenty-four years as a bivocational pastor, lovingly ministering to the people and making beautiful cabinetry and furniture. We need to revive this kind of flexible creativity in our institutional systems of call. In the coming years of ever-increasing marginal status for the mainline church, pastors will need proactive imaginations for constructing their lives and family economies.

The most effective means of change are not coming from top-down models where church judicatories change their polities to respond to small-church needs. The most effective and transforming influences are the proactive, creative initiatives of local lay leaders and ministers. Some lay leaders choose to search for pastoral leadership in innovative ways. Some choose to become trained in theology and the Bible and provide the leadership themselves. Some pastors make intentional decisions to stay in their small churches and ignore the career ladder. Some pastors initiate contact with other small churches in order to work cooperatively. The reality is that many denominational judicatories are not always in a position to initiate these kinds of changes. Supporting this kind of creativity would be better for these local settings and for the judicatories.

Surely more options and different models can be discovered when lay leaders and pastors exercise together their gifts of imagination and creativity. Many small-church pastors already look for outside sources of income. This approach challenges our traditional professional assumptions that the church can and will supply it all. The "road less traveled" of pastoring a small church is not an upwardly mobile career ladder for clergy—but it is wonderful work. And it may just change a pastor's heart and mind about what is most important. Financial creativity is necessary in order to do this work, and in the coming decades, I believe this will be true for many more congregations and their pastors, not only the peripheral rural and urban ones.

In my own family the rewards of reordering our lives have been remarkably satisfying for Amy and me as well as for our children. We are both fully engaged in following our callings, one as an educator and the other as a pastor. I continue to discover fresh energy, intelligence, imagination, and love for the work that I do and also for reaching out to other small-church clergy and congregations. My family's work feels in harmony and not in competition with our primary calling to follow Jesus Christ. I am sure that the model we have developed for our family will not become a new norm. But now is the time for a variety of models to be the new norm.

My work allows generous room for attending to my other personal callings in life. Whether it is hiking with my kids along the Blue Ridge, enjoying a music program with Amy at the college, preparing a meal for neighbor friends, visiting with my mother and sisters in North Carolina, learning how to side a house with cedar shake shingling, writing an article for a journal, working on a presbytery project, or helping to set up for a Celtic music concert at the public library, I find all these parts of my life to constitute a wonderful whole. They are not in competition with one another; rather they are mutually fulfilling. Yes, the cost of our simplified lives is that we have to creatively and carefully manage our resources. But I'll take that challenge over not doing what I love.

As our mainline denominations continue to get smaller, we owe it to the next generation of pastoral candidates to help them imagine the many different possibilities for congregational ministry and the many different paths for doing it. If we cannot muster this kind of creativity ourselves, then we should at least be willing to listen when the next generation imagines it for us.

# CHAPTER 7

# *Imagination*

*Almighty God, Sun behind all suns, Soul behind all souls, show to us in everything we touch and in everyone we meet the continued assurance of thy presence round us, lest ever we should think thee absent. In all created things thou art there. In every friend we have, the sunshine of thy presence is shown forth. In every enemy that seems to cross our path, thou art there within the cloud to challenge us to love. Show to us the glory in the grey. Awake for us thy presence in the very storm till all our joys are seen as thee and all our trivial tasks emerge as priestly sacraments in the universal temple of thy love.*

George MacLeod, founder of the Iona Community[1]

*You can't depend on your eyes when your imagination is out of focus.*

Mark Twain, *A Connecticut Yankee in King Arthur's Court*[2]

I remember a coffee conversation with a wise and thoughtful colleague who was a great help early in my pastoral journey. We met for coffee on Wednesday mornings with a number of friends in the surrounding area. Usually, our conversations roamed wildly from the state of the church to theological perspectives to which movies to go see. On this particular grey, wet February morning, my mood was about as dark as the winter weather.

The weather kept others away that day. So Gil and I sat by ourselves, hunched over our big mugs of coffee. I was in a funk, because a meandering two-hour session meeting the night before had been a useless argument about how to fix a leak in the church roof caused by the freezing and thawing of February rains. I whined, "How in the world can anybody talk about a leak for two hours?" The conversation and ensuing argument over such a narrow matter were symbolic of how constricted and visionless the church could be—I thought. I do not remember how long I ranted on in my righteous indignation.

On this particular morning Gil abandoned the usual reflective listening practice that most pastors employ when faced with such self-absorption. When I finally stopped to take a breath from my diatribe, Gil slowly looked up from his coffee. He said, "You have a very small imagination." "I have a small imagination!" I retorted. Gil calmly replied, "You could help them imagine how working on a leaky roof might be a part of their service to the kingdom of God or you could patiently wait until they've completed this task. You can't ignore a leaky roof. The most important thing is what kind of imagination you bring to the discussion." I thought about his reflections for a moment and then asked him if he had seen any good movies lately. Today Gil still serves the same congregation; he has been there for twenty-plus years. Engaged pastors of small congregations who have been in the same place for a long time often approach ordinary matters with lively imaginations.

A revival of faithful imagination in the people of small churches is a powerful thing. New programs or long-range planning committees or mission studies can be helpful, but more than the programs themselves is the imagination and attention to the Spirit we bring to them. Reflecting on how imagination works and how church leaders can employ their own imaginations and inspire the imaginations of folks in the pews can be fruitful.

I remember another older colleague, a veteran of World War II, giving a valedictory sermon at the end of his forty-plus-year service as a pastor. He spoke of the medieval stone masons who had spent their entire lifetimes crafting a small bit of a cathedral. He imagined that they must have seen their work as building the kingdom of God. No doubt they knew that they were merely constructing a window archway or a portion of wall. But weren't the most blessed of them those who envisioned that their small efforts were given for the glory of God? They had not completed the work to be done, the entire cathedral; ultimate fulfillment rested in the hands of God. This pastor was looking back and imagining what his work had been, and he found a beautiful image to capture it. The challenge of imagination, however, is also looking forward and considering what may be.

Many years ago I had my first imaginings of the mountains as a congregation in worship. How had I hiked so many trails and not previously seen the way that these magnificent trees were lifting up their mighty arms in worship? That image became so fixed in my thoughts that I see it all the time now. I cannot shake it.

Likewise, an integral part of my work as a pastor is imagining the people where I serve according to the lively images I find in the Scriptures. Here are the very children of the eternal God, Jesus's own brothers and sisters. They are the body of the risen Christ; the hands, feet, arms, and eyes of the loving Lord of all, reaching out to touch and heal God's beloved, broken world. Wendell Berry writes, "As the word [imagination] itself suggests, it is the power to make us *see*, moreover, things that without it would be unseeable. In one of its aspects it is the power by which we sympathize."[3]

One weekday afternoon I was sitting in the sanctuary picturing the different folks of the church, where they sat, and the families that surrounded them. I moved from one pew to the next and recalled the people, praying for them and thinking about what they were doing during the week. I didn't hear Beth as she was sneaking down the aisle. She plopped down loudly next to me on the pew, chuckling and smiling as she looked out over the pews. She obviously knew what I was doing, because she started in without any hesitation. "It helps to be able to see people. I do that almost every Sunday morning before worship starts. I picture all the people who have been here, especially those who were older when I was a kid. Now they're long gone, but they're still a part of us. To know that they still live with God helps me in my faith today." I asked Beth to tell me who she saw, and she went around the room and shared the names and stories of people in her mind's eye.

Sometimes I have imagined that the little, white clapboard church where I serve, tucked away in the hills of the old mining community of Pico, is the very center of the universe. I can see the New Jerusalem coming down from heaven and arriving in this little Appalachian hollow. I can see the elderly warily peeking out from their windows. I can see the children running and cheering along the road, straining to see through the treetops, and the cattle across the creek lifting up their heads from the hillside to witness heaven and earth in the first moment of becoming one. It's an outrageous image.

But it's really no more outrageous than the thought of an eternal God taking on flesh and walking along the Galilean hillsides.

Imagination is the creativity of heart, spirit, and mind that fuels the ongoing daily work of pastoral ministry in this special corner of God's world. Imagination is the prayerful interior work that helps me see what is really going on, not so much dreaming things up but rather being open to what could be.

Jesus used parables to open the eyes of his disciples to the surprising, upside-down ways of God, helping them imagine God's kingdom. Stories about sowers sowing seed, about weeds among the wheat, about mustard seeds, about hidden treasure and priceless pearls all shed light on that great reality that was opening up in their midst and was yet to come. Jesus's mind must have often wandered as he spent time alone in prayer, perhaps imagining these down-to-earth images as prisms through which one could glimpse the kingdom. When the disciples asked why Jesus spoke in parables, he answered by quoting the prophet Isaiah: "'This people's heart has grown dull, and their ears are hard of hearing, and they have shut their eyes; so that they might not look with their eyes, and listen with their ears, and understand with their heart and turn—and I would heal them.' But blessed are your eyes, for they see, and your ears, for they hear" (Matt. 13:15–16).

Jesus brought his disciples along amid the tasks of his ministry. Of course they had much to do. He gathered them and challenged them to follow him. He healed the blind and the lame. He sent his disciples out and instructed them how to carry out ministry in his name. He taught them in the prose of instruction and correction. He put them out on a limb in a crowd of five thousand, and said, "They need not go away;

you give them something to eat" (Matt. 14:16). He challenged the heavy-handedness of the Pharisees and Sadducees in the disciples' presence. And all the while, he stoked the embers of imagination to help them see what he was doing and envision the kingdom of God embodied in his very presence.

The poetry of trees, fruit, broods of vipers, vineyard keepers, wedding banquets, fig trees, and bridesmaids all shined a light on the tasks of his ministry and his journey to the cross. He used his vivid imagination to help his disciples see the surprising ways of God. Doing the tasks of ministry was not enough. If that service were the entirety of God's vision, they would have been thoroughly unprepared to see the shattering wonder of Easter morning. And even with the benefit of Jesus's imaginative teaching, that wonder was terribly difficult for the disciples to see. And even then, it was only the women who first saw.

I am grateful that the time and space of a small church allow me to exercise my imagination. Here, life's margins are generous enough for me to tromp through the woods and let my mind and spirit prayerfully wander. Here I have enough room to sit in the sanctuary and remember God's people by name. This "work" is integral to the tasks of ministry. For by it I bring not just more ideas but, more importantly, greater love to the tasks of writing sermons, visiting parishioners in the hospital and at home, moderating session meetings, and teaching Sunday school. While the tasks and the skills are important, I can bring nothing greater to my work than love. And I cannot conjure it through my own resolve. While love is an act of will, it involves the whole person—heart, soul, mind, and strength. And my only hope is the liveliness of the Spirit bringing life to the tasks of love. Where I often find the Spirit dancing is through the creativity of imagination.

I have found that exercising imagination bears much fruit in the rural, peripheral settings of the small congregations I have served. Using the gift of imagination is one way I serve and strengthen folks for being the people of God. Stories and images from the Scriptures and from everyday life become the prisms through which they can envision themselves as active participants in the kingdom of God. When images from television and the commercial world minimize the significance of their place, imagination becomes all the more important for seeing things from a livelier perspective.

But now let me get back to our situation in the larger church, because I have found in more central places a resistance to this imaginative work. I return to our anxious predicament of mainline Protestant church—numerical decline—and our fear for what the future holds for our shrinking denominations as we are becoming smaller. What role is imagination playing in our many deliberations about our current situation?

Much creativity is going on right now, even if some of it is a very anxious creativity. We are seeing the creativity of doing church differently in order to adapt to the changes of an emerging future. We are seeing the creativity of new denominational programs to try to regain lost numbers. We are seeing the creativity of those leaving old denominations they see as unfaithful in order to make new denominations of the likeminded. Some creativity springs from love and calling. Some creativity comes from fear and dread.

We are also seeing new, anxious images for what pastors should be and do. These out-of-focus images remind me that the work of imagination is not an ethereal, otherworldly endeavor done by poets in their lofty writing cells. Images for who pastors are and what we are doing remain necessary for the everyday, tough, down-to-earth decisions we make in ministry. When we fail to draw on lively and life-giving images, then images from the overbearing, dominant culture will fill the void. One new image now used quite unapologetically is the pastor as entrepreneur. I'm sure that the idea of pastor as entrepreneur is meant to stress the need for creativity. We might, however, want to ask what kind of creativity is communicated by this image, because it is hard not to see in it the idea of the pastor as the compulsive competitor for customers in a declining market share. When you're skating on thin ice, speed up! It is hardly an image that evokes love of God and neighbor. It doesn't bring God to mind at all. When parishioners hear that the pastor is an entrepreneur, they naturally conclude that the church is a business. Or maybe it is the other way around. When ministers conclude that the church is a business, then they become entrepreneurs.

This image has become widely used in the church. I find it difficult and uncomfortable raising this point, because I know many excellent, faithful leaders who are now using this language of entrepreneurship when talking about church leadership. But I still think it is a mistake. Why are we using market images when megaglobal business so dominates American life today with an overwhelming, monolithic voice proclaiming that the only answer to every problem is to get faster, get bigger, get richer? Can we imagine Isaiah using images from the overbearing, dominating Babylonian empire to inspire God's people to take up the long journey on the desert highway back to Israel? Those ancient, wise crafters of Old Testament stories did use a powerful image from Babylon, but this image wasn't one for the covenant people to imitate. The Tower of Babel was a creative image that critiqued a sick central culture that was using its power not for serving the good purposes of God but rather for dominating the cultures of those on the periphery.

What is lost in our rush to find the solution to our decline is the exercise of a lively faith imagination. We make little room and little space for imagining together where and what God may be up to in our changing world. From the outside we appear to be frantic workers striving to look busy, lest our absentee boss should show up on the job. If we could just cobble together a thousand new programs and projects, then maybe one of them might bear fruit and God will bless us again with success. I hear time and again in larger meetings of the church, "Let's just do something. We aren't doing anything." It makes me think that our new motto should be "Git 'er done." What we are doing and how it might exhibit the kingdom of God seems to be of less concern. Yet what I am longing for are more opportunities for the people of God to imagine together what God is doing now.

To ponder what is so hard to see we will need many imaginations. It is daunting work to try to describe what one does not know for sure. The chances are good that someone trying to see and describe will be quite wrong. I think the chances for getting a clearer glimpse would be better with many people imagining together and letting the Holy Spirit work among us.

Let me dare risk adding my imaginings to all those who are straining to see. I have imagined that God is the one who is making us smaller. What if God is the one shrinking the size and numbers of our denominations? Could it even be a possibility that God would do such a thing? Maybe it's not just the changes going on in our culture. Maybe it's not just demographic trends that make mainline Protestantism less attractive to consumers. Maybe it's not just our own failings and unfaithfulness that have brought on the judgment of a more marginal situation. Or maybe it is all these things and more through which God is making us smaller. If God is behind all this and in all this, how would it change the way we see things?

I suspect our answer to that question will depend in large part on whether we can imagine that God uses small things for heavenly purposes. Our sacred stories give us plenty of precedent for God's penchant to use small things. For those who can imagine that God is still using small things today, there remains great hope, because the wily ways of the Holy Spirit breathe life even where we are not looking for life.

Jesus said, "The kingdom of heaven is like treasure hidden in a field, which someone found and hid; then in his joy he goes and sells all that he has and buys that field" (Matt. 13:44). I imagine that God delights in hiding treasure in country fields rather than in imperial courts, in mangers and stables, along the well-worn paths of shepherds, making it fall like manna dew on his pilgrim people wandering in the wilderness. So for friends who are finding themselves in a new place on the periphery and adjusting to smaller scale and diminishing budgets, it's okay. Do not be afraid. God is here on the periphery too. And God's goodness and abundance abounds. The periphery is a surprisingly good and blessed place to rediscover the joy and the treasure that is worth everything.

My imaginings are that God is the one who is behind our decline in status, size, wealth, and influence. What if we were to let our attachment to these things go? What if we were to let our daydreams of recapturing them go? If we did, then we might be able to join what God is doing, because the Holy Spirit is the only guarantee of life on the other side of our past successes. If God is making us smaller, then we are being invited to die to what has been, and our only hope is that God's Spirit will be our font of life. If this is what is happening, then couldn't this be the moment for rediscovering our passion for ministry? We need not be anxiously looking over our shoulder for the culture's approval or someone else's pat on the back. We need only be attending to the people and places right in front of us, right where we live, to find the presence of the risen Lord of all creation.

What if the great God of Easter morning is doing a new thing in our midst and we simply need the eyes to see?

When we strain the eyes of our hearts to see a small, marginal congregation in a sympathetic light, then new attachments start to form. The work of seeing in a new way is the beginning of understanding. It is the beginning of love. This careful, loving, attentive work serves small congregations well and helps them to flourish. May the Spirit continue to move among us, helping us to see, helping us to love.

# Notes

## Chapter 1: Periphery

1. Muriel Earley Sheppard, *Cabins in the Laurel* (Chapel Hill: University of North Carolina Press, 1935), 236.
2. Wendell Berry, *The Way of Ignorance* (Washington, DC: Shoemaker and Hoard, 2005), 113.
3. Ibid., 113–14.
4. Robert W. Lynn and James W. Fraser, "Images of the Small Church in American History," in *Small Churches Are Beautiful*, ed. Jackson W. Carroll (San Francisco: Harper & Row, 1977), 7–8.
5. Anthony C. Pappas, *Vital Ministry in the Small-Membership Church: Healthy Esteem* (Nashville: Discipleship Resources, 2002), 10.
6. Debby Applegate, *The Most Famous Man in America: The Biography of Henry Ward Beecher* (New York: Doubleday Broadway, 2006), 202.

## Chapter 2: Simplicity

1. "The Church and Its Confessions," in *The Constitution of the Presbyterian Church (USA), Part II, Book of Order, 2009–2011* (Louisville: Office of the General Assembly, 2009), ch. 2, G-2.0500a.3.
2. *The Bill McKibben Reader: Pieces from an Active Life* (New York: Holt Paperbacks, 2008), 45.

## Chapter 3: Limits

1. Mother Teresa, in Dorothy S. Hunt, ed., *Love, A Fruit Always in Season: Daily Meditations by Mother Teresa* (San Francisco: Ignatius Press, 1987), 121.
2. "Table 15," in General Assembly Mission Council Comparative Statistics, 2010, Presbyterian Church (USA) website, http://gamc. pcusa.org/ministries/research/statistics-reports-and-articles/.
3. Pat Miller, "The Good Neighborhood: Identity and Community through the Commandments," in *Character and Scripture: Moral Formation, Community and Biblical Interpretation*, ed. William P. Brown (Grand Rapids: Eerdmans, 2002), 56.
4. Ibid.
5. Carl S. Dudley, *Making the Small Church Effective* (Nashville: Abingdon Press, 1978), 75.
6. Wendell Berry, *What Are People For?* (New York: North Point Press, 1996), 9.

## Chapter 4: Creation

1. J. Philip Newell, *Celtic Prayers from Iona* (New York/ Mahwah, NJ: Paulist Press, 1997), 39.
2. John Muir, *My First Summer in the Sierra* (Boston: Houghton Mifflin, 1911), 110.
3. Kathleen Norris, *Dakota: A Spiritual Geography* (Boston: Houghton Mifflin, 1993), 21.
4. Wendell Berry, *The Way of Ignorance* (Washington, DC: Shoemaker and Hoard, 2005), 85.
5. *New World Dictionary of American English* (Cleveland: Simon & Schuster, 1988), s.v. "sustain."
6. Ellen F. Davis, *Scripture, Culture, and Agriculture: An Agrarian Reading of the Bible* (Cambridge, UK: Cambridge University Press, 2009), 66–79.

## Chapter 5: Belonging

1. Blaise Pascal "Of the Means of Belief," Section IV in *Thoughts*, The Harvard Classics, Vol. 48 (P. F. Collier & Son, 1910), 274.
2. Anthony G. Pappas, *Vital Ministry in the Small-Membership Church: Healthy Esteem* (Nashville: Discipleship Resources, 2002), 10.
3. Task Force on Ministry to the Small Church to the 113th General Assembly of the Presbyterian Church in the United States, "Strengthening the Small Church for Its Mission" (The Presbyterian Church in the United States, 1974).
4. "Heidelberg Catechism," in *The Book of Confessions* (Louisville: Presbyterian Distribution, 2002.

## Chapter 6: Bills

1. Robert Frost, *The Road Not Taken: A Selection of Robert Frost's Poems*, ed. Louis Untermeyer (New York: Henry Holt, 1971), 130.
2. Carol Howard Merritt, *Tribal Church: Ministering to the Missing Generation* (Herndon, VA: Alban Institute, 2007), 39–40.

## Chapter 7: Imagination

1. MacLeod, quoted in J. Philip Newell, *Listening for the Heartbeat of God: A Celtic Spirituality* (New York/Mahwah, NJ: Paulist Press, 1997), 87.
2. Mark Twain, *The Writings of Mark Twain, Vol. 16: A Connecticut Yankee in King Arthur's Court* (1889; New York: Harper & Brothers, 1899), 398.
3. Wendell Berry, *Imagination in Place* (Berkeley, CA: Counterpoint, 2010), 186–87.